RECORDER TECHNIQUE

Recorder Technique

BY

A. ROWLAND-JONES

London
OXFORD UNIVERSITY PRESS
NEW YORK   TORONTO

Oxford University Press, Ely House, London W. 1

GLASGOW NEW YORK TORONTO MELBOURNE WELLINGTON
CAPE TOWN IBADAN NAIROBI DAR ES SALAAM LUSAKA ADDIS ABABA
DELHI BOMBAY CALCUTTA MADRAS KARACHI LAHORE DACCA
KUALA LUMPUR SINGAPORE HONG KONG TOKYO

ISBN 0 19 318604 7

First published 1959
Fifth impression (corrected) 1969
Seventh impression 1973

Printed in Great Britain

To Christina, my best pupil

CONTENTS

I	THE HISTORY OF THE RECORDER	1
II	THE RECORDER'S REPERTOIRE	10
III	KINDS OF RECORDERS: CHOOSING AN INSTRUMENT	29
IV	BEGINNING TO PLAY THE RECORDER	41
V	BREATHING	53
VI	TONGUING	59
VII	INTONATION	66
VIII	ALTERNATIVE FINGERINGS	74
IX	HIGH NOTES	92
X	VOLUME	98
XI	TONE	104
XII	ORNAMENTATION	112
XIII	PRACTICE	122
XIV	PERFORMANCE	128
	SOME RECORDERS AVAILABLE IN THE UNITED KINGDOM	136
	SUPPLEMENT TO CHAPTER II	141
	TABLE OF NORMAL FINGERINGS	148
	INDEX	149

ACKNOWLEDGEMENTS

This book is based upon a series of articles printed in *The Recorder News*, the journal of the Society of Recorder Players, and I should like to thank the editor, Mr. C. Kenworthy, for his assistance and for agreeing that the articles should appear in book form. I also wish to acknowledge the help and encouragement that has been given me by Mr. Edgar Hunt, who read and criticized the book before publication, Dr. J. G. Neville of Liverpool, who looked through the proofs, Mr. Layton Ring, who helped me with Chapters III and XII, Mr. Lyndesay G. Langwill (Honorary Treasurer of the Galpin Society) who gave me access to his *Index of Musical Wind Instrument Makers*, the staff of the Library of King's College, Newcastle upon Tyne, and Miss Jane Branson of Newcastle who, as an enthusiastic pupil, unwittingly gave me considerable help in discovering and solving problems of technique and its application. The information on makes of recorders could not have been compiled had not the following so freely given of their time and assistance: Mr. Carl Dolmetsch and the staff of his workshops at Haslemere, Miss Marylin Wailes, Mr. C. F. Pringsheim of 'Pro Arte Musica', and the staffs of Messrs. Schott and Co. Ltd., John E. Dallas & Sons, Ltd., Boosey and Hawkes, Ltd., and J. G. Windows, Ltd., of Newcastle upon Tyne. I should also like to record my grateful thanks to Dr. Walter Bergmann who, in his classes at Morley College, taught me a great deal about recorder playing and about music.

Readers of this book are advised to purchase the same author's *A Practice Book for the Treble Recorder*, which is published by Oxford, in which exercises taken from the recorder's repertoire are provided to elucidate problems of technique and interpretation, and *Scales, Arpeggios, and Exercises for the Recorder* by Margaret and Robert Donington.

THE HISTORY OF THE RECORDER

It is hard to say exactly how old a musical instrument the recorder is. End-blown whistles or flutes in which sound is made by means of a notch or 'fipple' existed in pre-historic times: they were heard in the caves of the Dordogne, in the mountains of Peru, and on the banks of the Nile; in the rites of paganism their music protected the priest from the distraction of more mundane sounds. Primitive flutes appear to have depended on 'overblowing' to produce a practicable compass of notes. A narrow-bore flute with three holes (such as the tabor-pipe) can play two octaves by using four degrees of breath-pressure, while a flute with six holes (such as the flageolet or the 'tin whistle') can produce two octaves with two breath-pressures. The recorder, however, has eight holes, one of which, the thumb-hole, is used partly as a 'speaker' to facilitate the formation of notes in the second octave without the need for stronger breath-pressure; a 'speaker' device is also used on the clarinet and the oboe. Despite its apparent simplicity, the recorder is therefore the most highly developed of end-blown fipple-flutes.

Evidence from illuminated manuscripts or from carvings in Gothic cathedrals cannot be relied upon to tell when the use of the octaving thumb-hole on the fipple-flute was discovered, and when, therefore, the first true recorder came into being. Medieval representations of wind instruments are seldom in close detail, and even the best representation is unlikely to reveal the essential thumb-hole on the underside as well as the seven finger-holes on top. Canon F. W. Galpin, in his *Old English Instruments of Music* (London, 1910), claims that the earliest illustration of the recorder is given in a twelfth-century psalter in the University Library, Glasgow; the only recorder-like attribute, however, is the puzzlement shown by the player who is obviously having some difficulty in working out the fingering. Canon Galpin also shows a curious creature from a thirteenth-century manuscript in the Bodleian Library, half man and half cock, playing an instrument of the fipple-flute family which may be a recorder. Although there is a tradition that eight-holed fipple-flutes originated amongst the Italian peasantry in the fifteenth century no instruments are extant to prove it, as the oldest instruments still in existence date from the beginning of the sixteenth century.

The word 'recorder' first appeared in a number of monkish dictionaries and commentaries as far back as the end of the thirteenth century, generally as a translation of Latin words meaning, vaguely, 'flute'. The word is associated with the verb 'to record' which refers to the warbling noises made by birds, particularly young birds in the nest, and the name might have been transferred to the musical instrument because of its being used to teach birds to sing (see *The Bird Fancyer's Delight*, ed. S. Godman, pub. Schott). Alternatively the connexion may have been simply in the similarity of the recorder's tone-quality to bird-song, for the word was used for bird-song generally, as in Jonson's madrigal in *The Triumphs of Oriana* (1603)— 'Then tune to us, sweet bird, thy shrill recorder'. Another possibility is in the use of 'to record' in the sense of 'to sing softly' or 'to hum', and this might have led to 'la flûte douce' being termed a 'recorder'. There are infrequent references in medieval literature to an instrument called the recorder, but they do not provide conclusive evidence as to the age of the eight-holed instrument as we now know it, for the word may have been used originally for other fipple-flutes. On the other hand, true recorders may easily have been known by some other name such as 'doucet', 'pipe', or 'flute'. It is quite possible that Chaucer's Squire, who was 'syngynge or floytynge al the day' played an early descant recorder (provided the wind over the Kentish Downs was not too strong).

The earliest conclusive documentary evidence for the existence of the recorder comes from the same period as the surviving instruments. This is Virdung's *Musica getutscht* (Basle, 1511) in which a quartet of recorders is accurately illustrated, the thumb-hole being clearly indicated. Later writers, such as Agricola (1528), Ganassi (1535), Praetorius (1619), and Mersenne (1636), illustrate both recorders and transverse flutes, under various names. They all show a complete family of recorders: Praetorius mentions eight different sizes, including a contrabass in F, while Mersenne describes an even bigger instrument, a contrabass (possibly in D) with the lowest holes operated by pedals. Mersenne's recorders are called 'flute d'Angleterre', 'flute a neuf trous' (see p. 42), or 'flute douce', and an entry in Palsgrave's English-French vocabulary of 1530 reading 'Recorder a pype fleute a ix neufte trous' makes it clear that the word 'recorder' in the sixteenth century had exactly the meaning it has today. Outside England there was no single word to differentiate the recorder from the equally popular transverse flute, and confusion inevitably arises.

In Tudor times the recorder was a much favoured instrument. Entries in the royal accounts show that Henry VII gave twenty shillings 'To Arnolde pleyer at recorders' and, on the 14th of February, 1492, 'To the childe that playeth on the records, 20 shillings'. Henry VIII, we are told by Holinshed (*Chronicle* for 1510), exercised himself daily 'in shooting, singing, dansing, wrestling, casting of the barre, plaieing at the recorders, flute, virginals, in setting of songs and making of ballads'; the inventory of his wardrobe includes a magnificent collection of recorders—one item reads 'a Case coured w^t crimeson vellat havinge locke and all other garnishements to the same of Silver gilte w^t viij recorders of Ivorie in the same Case the twoo bases garnisshed w^t Silver and guilte'. Recorders took part in the great reception prepared for Queen Elizabeth at Kenilworth in 1575, at which the boy Shakespeare may have been an onlooker.

Elizabethan and Jacobean dramatists made use of the recorder for incidental music. We know that the visiting players at Elsinore had recorders with them, in all likelihood to play while the dumb-show was proceeding, for flutes or recorders are called for in exactly such contexts in Gascoigne's *Jocasta* (1575) and in Norton and Sackville's *Gorboduc* (1565), the first English tragedy. Marston, who was most particular about the incidental music to his plays, twice explicitly requires recorders in the stage-directions to *Sophonisba* (1606) : in Act III he asks for 'Organ mixt with recorders' and in Act V, Scene i 'Organ and re-corders play to a single voice'. A play that belongs to the Shakespeare apocrypha, *The Two Noble Kinsmen* (1634), gives a direction for 'Still music of records', which, taken in conjunction with the reference to 'Still flutes' in *Jocasta*, makes one suspect that the stage direction 'still music' was always a cue for recorders. J. S. Manifold, in his interesting book on *The Music in English Drama* (London, 1956), proves that the recorder, with its ethereal and solemn tone, was used almost exclusively in 'other-world' contexts—scenes of death, miracles, unearthly joy, or to denote the presence of a Christian or pagan deity. This connotation persisted into the Restoration period, for Pepys provides evidence that the recorder was used in a revival of Massinger's *Virgin Martyr* for 'the wind-musique when the angel comes down'. Dryden calls for recorders in *Albion and Albanius* (1685), an entertainment with many machine-fuls of gods in it, and Blow in *Venus and Adonis* (1685) uses recorders only in connexion with the gods in the opera, and never to accompany the mortals. The use of the recorder in pastoral scenes developed in Italy, but was not copied in England until Purcell's time. Bach uses the recorder both in other-worldly and in pastoral contexts.

The early Puritans listed players of the flute and the recorder—'pipers'—amongst the 'caterpillars of a common-wealth'. There is a curiously modern ring about the anecdote told in Foxe's *Book of Martyrs* (1563) about the Puritan Bilney, who was in residence at Trinity Hall, Cambridge: 'When Dr. Thurlby, afterwards bishop, the scholar living in the chamber underneath him, would play upon his recorder (as he would often do) he [i.e. Bilney] would resort strait to his prayer.' It may be significant that in *Paradise Lost* it is the Satanic hosts who 'move In perfect *Phalanx* to the *Dorian* mood Of Flutes and soft Recorders' (Book I, 549–51). Milton, however, was certainly not amongst those few die-hard Puritans who are reputed to have despised music : like most Englishmen of that time he was brought up in a thoroughly musical atmosphere in a country renowned in Europe for the quality of its music and musicians—and especially its wind-players. Milton's father was an excellent composer and the instruments he wrote for included 'softlie touchd recordes'. The effect of eleven years of Commonwealth was to freeze the development of professionalism in music (although there is evidence that one at least of the six recorder players employed by Charles I received arrears of pay during the Commonwealth) and to make the recorder a domestic instrument.

Nevertheless, hazy evidence does point to a decline in the popularity of the recorder in England during the second quarter of the seventeenth century, for the chamber-music of that period is mainly for viols, and is less suited to the kind of treatment suggested by Holborne (d. 1602) who wrote alternatively 'for Viols, Violins or other [=otherwise] Musicall Wind Instruments'. By the time of the Restoration the recorder was so little known in London society that the same instrument under a different name—the 'flûte douce'—was brought from the French court as a novelty. A situation existed similar to what happened in eighteenth-century architecture when fashionable and consciously 'gothick' temples were built by expensive architects in the gardens of landowners at the same time as local stonemasons were building traditional and unconsciously gothic churches in the landowners' villages. Fashions change quickly, and in 1679 Shadwell was writing of ' matters in France'—'Wit and Women are quite out of Fashion; so are Flutes Doux and Fidlers; Drums and Trumpets are their only Musick' (*A True Widow*, I, i), and in the same year Hudgebut, in the first of a series of recorder tutors which appeared from then until well into the eighteenth century,[1] feels that it is necessary to extol the recorder at the expense of the flageolet which was the most popular of amateur instruments in the early days of

[1] E.g. John Hudgebut, *Lessons for the Rechorder* (1679); John Banister, *The Most Pleasant Companion* (1681); Humphrey Salter, *The Genteel Companion* (1683); Henry Playford and John Carr (pub.), *The Delightful Companion, or Choice new lessons for the Recorder or Flute* (1684); Hare and Walsh (pub.), *The Compleat Flute-Master* (1690); Hotteterre-le-Romain, *Principes de*

the Restoration (Pepys was an enthusiastic player). In 1684 John Carr writes, 'This Delightful Companion the Pipe Recorder hath been for a long time out of use, but now it's beginning to be in greater repute than it ever was before. . . .' As its popularity gained ground both in amateur music and in opera, the recorder became known simply as the 'flute', for the keyless transverse flute was almost in disuse in England (though certainly not in France) up to about 1700. The one-keyed transverse flute was introduced into England early in the eighteenth century, and took upon itself the title of 'traversa' (used by Handel) or 'German' as against 'English' flute. It was not until mid-century that the word 'flute' came to have the meaning of 'transverse flute' once again, at which stage the moribund recorder was dubbed the 'common flute'. 'Flauto' in all music published from the Restoration up to the middle of the eighteenth century refers, therefore, solely to the recorder.

Even before the publication of Longman and Broderip's tutor in 1779 or later, the 'common flute' was far less common than its name implied, if it is fair to judge the popularity of an instrument by the amount of music written for it. The German flute gained ground from mid-century onwards because at last steps were being taken to remedy the defects of the key-less or one-keyed instruments. On the transverse flute the player has far more control over tone-formation than the fipple-flute, and consequently the transverse flute is capable of wider variations in volume and tone-quality than the recorder, making it more flexible in expression. The cross-fingerings used on the key-less flute to obtain notes outside the basic diatonic major scale of the instrument, however, strangle tone far more than similar cross-fingerings do on the recorder, with the result that it was difficult to obtain anything approaching tonal evenness in music written outside the basic scale (usually

la flûte traversière ou flûte d'Allemagne, de la flûte à bec ou flûte douce, et du hautbois (1707); *The Modern Music Master*—'Directions for Playing on the Flute' (1731); John Tyther, *The Complete Flute Master* (?1740+); J. Sadler, *The Muses Delight* (1754); Longman and Broderip (pub.), *Compleat Instructions for the Common Flute* (?1779+).

D major) of the flute. The tone-quality of a key-less flute being played in E flat major is distinctly stifled and unpleasant, and, partly because of the even spacing of the holes, intonation would be deplorable unless the flute was played by an expert: composers from Alessandro Scarlatti to Mozart testify that the transverse flute was frequently played out of tune. From 1760 onwards irrational conservative objections to the piercing of extra holes covered by closed-standing keys in the one-keyed flute were being overcome and the process was under way of gradually improving the instrument up to the mechanical perfection achieved by Boehm. The addition of key-work to the recorder would have had little effect in making it louder, giving it more tonal variety, or increasing its agility in fast music or remote keys; moreover the recorder leaves only a thumb and a little finger free to manipulate keys while the six-holed flute has twice those potentialities. Even before 1760 transverse flutes were ousting recorders from the orchestra because of their ability to produce louder volume.   Fashion, too, had something to do with it, for in the late eighteenth century proficiency on the German flute was the mark of a gentleman: the 'Gentlemen's Concerts' founded in Manchester in 1774 began as a band of twenty-six flutes. Anomalies of notation of recorder music may have sped the instrument's demise, for recorder music was always curiously represented—in the seventeenth century by dot tablature in which the player read fingerings, not notes of music, and later by the use of the French violin clef with G at the bottom of the stave. All this meant that recorder players did not have easy access to music written for other instruments or for the voice, and music publishers would hesitate to stipulate alternative instrumentation for a sonata (e.g. 'for violin or German flute') if it meant engraving additional parts. The change in the style of music towards the sentimental and romantic would also favour the flute rather than the recorder, for in tone-quality the recorder is quite the least sensuous of all wind instruments. Its pure and dispassionate tone may equally well account for its return to favour in modern times.

In 1911, when Christopher Welch published his *Six*

Lectures on the Recorder,[1] a volume to which any writer on the recorder must acknowledge a great debt, the recorder was spoken of as 'extinct'. Yet by 1919 Arnold Dolmetsch had produced the first modern recorders, and in 1926 a full consort of recorders with bass was played at the Haslemere Festival.[2] The awakening of interest in old music brought with it a desire to hear this music played as nearly as possible as the composer intended it to sound. At the same time the pioneering work of Edgar Hunt and other members of the Society of Recorder Players (founded October 1937) to introduce the recorder as an educational instrument in schools was producing the most gratifying results, and in Germany the recorder had been taken up as a folk instrument, unfortunately with 'simplified' fingering, since abandoned. An increased interest in music generally, perhaps as a result of the war, made many previously unmusical people wish to learn to play an instrument, and the recorder, good plastic models of which were being mass-produced during and after the war, commended itself because it is cheap, uncomplicated, and easy to play in the elementary stages.

The present state of the recorder is that it is probably the most played of wind instruments and certainly the least practised, with the result that the standard of playing is low. The slovenly breath control, careless fingering, and deplorable intonation that seem to satisfy many recorder players would make the average amateur flautist or oboist blench: a child learning to play the violin knows more about the mechanics and potentialities of his instrument

[1] The first three of Christopher Welch's lectures have been reprinted by O.U.P. (1961), together with an introduction by Edgar Hunt. These three lectures are those of most interest to recorder players; they are entitled 'Literary errors on the subject of the recorder', 'Tone and effect of the recorder', and 'Hamlet and the recorder'. Edgar Hunt's book *The Recorder and its Music* (Herbert Jenkins, 1962) is mainly historical and contains a useful bibliography.

[2] The full story of the recorder revival may be read in Mabel Dolmetsch's book, *Personal Recollections of Arnold Dolmetsch* (London, 1958), in articles by Edgar Hunt in *Grove's Dictionary* and in the *Proceedings* of the Royal Musical Association 1948–9, pp. 49–51, and by Carl Dolmetsch in *Music and Letters*, 1941, pp. 67–74.

after a year of instruction than most supposedly competent recorder teachers ever get to know about theirs. Even some of the best players are not as good as they should be. There are recitalists who slow down when they come to difficult bits in a sonata and who fluff and scamper passage-work that is the daily bread of the orchestral wind-player. Critics reviewing recorder concerts speak of technical imperfections and tonal monotony when they ought to be concentrating on the music and its interpretation. How can the recorder re-establish itself in the minds of players of other instruments, conductors, and composers, as a musical instrument as important as, say, the oboe or violin, its peers a hundred and fifty years ago, if the average standard of performance is not worthy of the music written for it? It is the aim of this book, by going back to first principles and giving comprehensive instruction, to encourage amateur players, some of whom may well be losing interest in the recorder for lack of proper guidance, to acquire a good enough technique to play music to their own, their colleagues', and their listeners' full satisfaction.

II

THE RECORDER'S REPERTOIRE

In this chapter the following abbreviations are used:

Bärenreiter	Ba
Boosey and Hawkes	Boos.
Breitkopf and Härtel	Br & H
'Corona' series (Möseler)	Cor
Deutscher Ricordi Verlag	DRV
Hinrichsen Edition	H
'Hortus Musicus' series (Bärenreiter)	HM
Moeck (obtainable from Schott)	Mk
Möseler (obtainable from Novello)	Mo
Musica Rara	MR
Nagel (including 'Musica Practica' series) (obtainable from Bärenreiter)	Na
'Musik-Archiv' series (Nagel)	N. Arch
Oxford University Press	OUP
Schott	S
'Antiqua' series (Schott)	S. Ant
'Archive' series (Schott)	S. Arch
Universal Edition ('Il flauto dolce' series)	U
'Zeitschrift für Spielmusik' (Moeck)	ZfS

Recorder players are recommended to obtain the catalogues of these publishers from their music dealers.

Medieval music

It was not until the end of the sixteenth century that composers became interested enough in instrumental tone-colour to wish to stipulate which instruments should play a piece, or a part, of music. In the Middle Ages, instruments generally only substituted for singers or helped out a vocal line, and any instrument was played on that happened to be at hand. Certain music intended for vigorous dancing, however, was played on instruments alone. Chaucer tells us (*House of Fame*, l. 1235) that 'pipers' played 'love-daunces, sprynges, and reyes' (round dances), and (*Romance of the Rose*, l. 4250) that 'floytes' played 'hornepipes of

Cornewaile' so there is some likelihood that the Provençal estampidas, the French estampies, and English dances such as the two thirteenth-century pieces in the British Museum (MS Douce 139) were, on occasions, played on a fipple-flute, possibly with six holes. This sort of music has an air of truth about it played on a descant recorder with tambourine accompaniment. Publications of medieval music include some solo estampies (ZfS 181), pieces by Dunstable and Dufay (S. Arch 55 and 11)—the latter's 'Ave Regina' is impressive on two bass recorders and a tenor, and 'Mediaeval Songs and Dances' edited for 2 D and Tr by Layton Ring (U). In the S. Ant. edition of the three-voice organa 'Benedicamus Domino' the editor advises on how to obtain something approaching the original sounds with modern instruments and voices. The volumes of 'Mediaeval Carols', 'The Eton Choirbook', and 'Dunstable's Complete Works' in the *Musica Britannica* series (Stainer and Bell) (nos. 4, 8, 10, 11, and 12) are most rewarding to recorder players: the recorders should double a vocal line in this music.

The Renaissance

There is untold wealth in the music of the early Renaissance. The best introduction to it is the *Liber Fridolini Sichery* (S), a collection dated 1500 of three-, four-, and five-part instrumental music by Flemish masters such as Josquin des Près (Luther's favourite composer), Okeghem, Agricola, Obrecht, and Isaac. Some fifty polyphonic pieces are contained in this book, nearly all of them being settings of then popular tunes: it is hard to know where to begin, but 'La alfonsina' by Jean Ghiselin is amongst the most attractive. There are six more Isaac quartets in HM 29, and other music of the period in ZfS 9, ZfS 58, and S. Arch 49, as well as two delightful books of two-part Bicinie (S. Ed. 2836 and HM 74). Much of the music of the Renaissance period ostensibly for voices was performed with voices and instruments mixed or by instruments alone. As late as 1619 Praetorius writes that in motets for two or more choirs, one of the choirs could be a consort of recorders instead of voices, and parts in Elizabethan madrigals were often played by instruments—'apt for voices or viols' is a phrase frequently found at the head of madrigal publications. Recorder players who are not singers, therefore, should not hesitate to regard the vocal music of Palestrina, Victoria, Sweelinck (see HM 75), Taverner, Tye, Byrd, etc., as legal territory; Dowland's 'Ayres for Four Voices' (*Musica Britannica* 6), for example, go well on recorders alone, and better in collaboration with singers.

This does not imply, however, that there is any dearth of Renaissance music intended for instruments only. All European countries were then producing music for organ and other keyboard instruments, for lute, and for instrumental ensembles, and the recorder player's repertoire is enriched by all this output, for a *lingua franca* of instrumentation persisted throughout the period and into the seventeenth century. Lute and viol music used the same tablature, and ensemble pieces such as Gabrieli's 'La Spiritata' were adapted for keyboard. Bassano's fantasias (1585) (HM 64) are for 'tre voci per cantar e sonar con ogni sorte d'Istrumenti', and a 'Battaglia per strumenti da fiato' by Annibale Padovano (1527–75) was performed on one occasion by eight 'tromboni', eight 'viole da arco', eight 'grandi flauti' (almost certainly bass recorders), one 'strumento da penna', one 'laute', and fourteen voices. The purist should feel no shame, therefore, in playing arrangements of Farnaby's virginal music (S. Arch 27), or of Johann Walther's organ Choral Preludes (ZfS 169)—indeed a consort of recorders probably sounds more like a Renaissance organ than a modern organ does.

The instrumental ensemble music of the later Renaissance can be played either by a recorder consort, or with a 'broken consort' of mixed instruments, the former being more appropriate to music of the latter half of the sixteenth century, as the building up of complete families of instruments of one kind took place gradually during the century. There is so much instrumental ensemble music of this period that it would be impracticable to attempt to mention all of it here: instead readers are recommended to refer to the appropriate sections of Gustave Reese's *Music in the Renaissance* (London, 1954: for Italian music see pp. 545–52, 566–70, French 563–6, 570–1, German 671–2, 711, and English 867–83),

and to Ernst Meyer's *English Chamber Music* (London, 1946).
In the following paragraphs a purely subjective attempt is
made to pick out the best and most typical music of the
period from current publications.

Of the vast amount of instrumental music produced in
Italy during the sixteenth century, the most attractive is
probably Gabrieli's with its exciting sonorities. Gabrieli
expected his music to be played on strong instruments such
as trombones and cornetts, but any mixed consort can
do justice to the four superb *Canzoni per sonar a 4* published by S. Ant. Apart from the canzoni the main purely
instrumental forms were the ricercare and the bicinia.
Palestrina's eight four-part *Ricercari sopra li Tuoni* (S. Ant)
belong to a calmer world than Gabrieli's pieces, but their
purity of form is in its own way just as exciting. Willaert's
three-part Ricercari (S. Ant) are rhythmically more complex than Palestrina's, and foreshadow the extended
Fantasia which became the vehicle of the most serious
musical thought of the late Renaissance (a parallel to the
nineteenth-century string quartet). Some excellent Italian
Fantasia music is published in Na. 564 and S. Arch. 72–4.
The two-part Bicinia were written mainly as exercises, but
those of Gastoldi (HM 23–4) transcend their purpose as
successfully as do Chopin's Etudes.

The comparative simplicity of the instrumental music
composed in France and the Low Countries after the
beginning of the sixteenth century may have been the
result of musicians being attracted to Italy in the same way
as they were to England in the early seventeenth century
when England was the acknowledged leader in the sphere
of instrumental music. Many a newly formed recorder
consort must be grateful, however, for the Attaignant
(1500) and Tielman Susato (1551) notebooks (S. Ed.
3758–9, 2435–6) and the Widman and Voelckel dances
(1600) (S. Ed. 2657). There is more music of this style,
generally based on courtly dance forms, in subscription
editions of such composers as Claude Gervaise (see also
H 1550 and Na MP 44–6) and Etienne du Tertre.

A Silesian employed at the court of Hungary, Thomas
Stoltzer (1450–1526), was the first composer of an extended

piece of instrumental music. His set of Fantasias in the eight modes 'Octo tonorum Melodiae' are full of superb sounds, but the S. Antiqua publication needs either a broken consort with two violas and cello or recorder players who can read the alto clef. Johann Walther's two-part fugues or, rather, canons, on the eight 'Tonos' (1542) (HM 63) are also interesting because the composer remarks that they may be played on any equal-voiced instruments, but especially 'tzincken' (cornetts). There are some excellent Bicinia by Rhau (1545) (ZfS 112) and Lassus (HM 18, 19: MR). Recommended publications of later German Renaissance music include the six-part Intradas from Hans Leo Hassler's 'Lustgarten', gay and simple music inviting varied 'orchestration' (HM 73), the dance suites of Schein (ZfS 43 and 49: S. Arch 44–5) and Melchior Frank (ZfS 28, 32: N. Arch 80: S. SRP 18), and the Canzone of Scheidt (HM 96 and 140) both of which, but especially the second, 'Super Intradam Aechiopicam', are bubbling with good spirits (for Scheidt see also ZfS 184 and N. Arch 137, 179, and 180). A wealth of German music of this period is published in the 'Corona' series: nos. 13 and 14 are dances by Michael Praetorius, many of which have fanciful names which assist in their interpretation, 50 includes a satisfying group of settings of 'In Dulci Jubilo' also by Praetorius, 49 is devoted to fugues by Hassler, and 44–8 contain various canzone, ricercari, fugues, and choral preludes, originally for organ. Taken on the whole, German music of this period appears to be four-square and extrovert, Italian music sinuous and passionate, and English graceful and melancholy.

One of the greatest enjoyments a recorder player can have is to be a member of a consort playing 'Lachrimae or Seaven Teares figured in Seaven Passionate Pavans, with divers other Pavans, Galiards and Almands' by John Dowland (1605) (OUP: S. Arch 19–25: Na 173), or Byrd's instrumental Fantasias arranged from E. H. Fellowes' complete edition of Byrd's works, Volume XVII (Stainer and Bell: also S. Arch 5, 7, 58, 64). Byrd's 'Browning' (S. Arch 58), a setting of a tune beginning 'The leaves be greene, the nuts be browne', was justifiably popular in his own day, and is delightful on five recorders provided the players have a good sense of rhythm. Schott's 'Archive' series has done much to remedy a previous shortage of Elizabethan consort music; it includes Michael East's 'Ayerie Fancies' (31–4, 75), numerous pieces by Anthony Holborne (17, 26, 50–2, 65 and SRP 13), Orlando Gibbons' Fantasias (10, 36, 37, 71; also Na 563 and 565, and S. Ant 'London Street-Cries'), two pieces by Deering (54), Fancies by Mico (66–8), and a Wilbye six-part Fantasia (43). Other essentials for the recorder-player's collection of Elizabethan music are the Morley two-part Canzonets (ed. Boalch-George Ronald, Oxford, 1950), and the In Nomines in HM 134. The setting of the In Nomine cantus firmus gave composers from Taverner to Purcell an opportunity to vie with each other in ingenuity and intensity of expression, and the HM volume contains seven of the hundred and fifty In Nomines extant, including Taverner's famous 'Trust' and 'Trye' In Nomines. Two superb four-part Fantasias by Orlando Gibbons are published by Stainer and Bell, as well as other pieces by Gibbons, Morley, and Tomkins and a useful little series called 'The Consort Player'. A short and perfect three-part Fantasy by Morley from *A Plaine & Easy Introduction to Practicall Musicke* (1597) is published by the Workers' Music Association. Three of Adson's 'Courtly Masquing Ayres Composed to 5. and 6. parts for Violins, Consorts and Cornets' (1621) are published by Universal, and two more by OUP. Arrangements for recorders of Elizabethan keyboard and lute music provide some of the happiest music for consorts. Particularly recommended are the five pieces in S. Arch 3, the Farnaby arrangements (27), and the Bull organ Ricercari (30), while 'Parthenia' (1611), and 'The Mulliner Book' (1545–85) (*Musica Britannica* 1 : S. Arch 6, 14) provide further material of high quality, even though the music may as a whole be less serious than that composed originally for instrumental ensemble.

The best source of English instrumental ensemble music of the seventeenth century is *Musica Britannica* 9, 'Jacobean Consort Music', together with the Scottish pieces in *Musica Britannica* 15. It is distressing to recorder players that much of this magnificently intellectual, slightly uncomfortable music can only be played to true effect on viols, and in choosing music of this period recorder consorts, even those with a great bass in C, must have regard to its suitability and the compass of the parts. It is better, however, to 'arrange' it or to play it in broken consort than to ignore it altogether, for the names of Ferrabosco, Jenkins, Ives (all three represented in H.D88), Coperario, Lupo, Ward, Hume, William Lawes, and Matthew Locke have been close to oblivion too long. A beginning on the music of this period can be made with a Jenkins trio (S. Arch 13), the Simpson suite and Lawes pieces in U., Hilton's 'Tricinia' (ZfS 87), and two Locke trios (S. Arch 9, and 'The Consort Player' 5). This serves to whet the appetite for the Locke four-part Suites (S. Ant), each in the form of an extended Fantasia, often with a slow introductory section, followed by a Courante, an Air (repeated in entirety softly), and a fast Sarabande. Consorts who dare to scale the summits may then attempt the last and greatest Fantasias, those of Purcell (Curwen: N. Arch 58, 113). Less skill is needed and an equal reward gained by those who discover Purcell's two In Nomines (N. Arch 113), one in six parts, the other in seven.

The Baroque era

If the legitimacy of playing Locke and Purcell Fantasias on recorders is somewhat in question, it is partly because from the middle of the sixteenth century onwards interest was growing in instrumental tone-colour and composers were beginning to write with definite instruments in mind. An early example of the recorder being used on a specific occasion is in music by Corteccia and Striggio for a dramatic representation in 1565, when a piece representing heavenly harmonies was played by four harpsichords, four viols, two sackbuts, two lutes, two tenor recorders, a flute, and a cornett (see Reese, op. cit., p. 569). Amongst the first composers to stipulate exact orchestration was the Italian Beaujoyeaux (*Ballet Comique de la Reine*, 1581), but he was soon followed by the early opera writers. Monteverdi in *Orfeo* calls for an orchestra of five 'viole da braccio', three 'chitarroni', two harpsichords, a double harp, a 'contra-basso di viola', and a 'flautino alla vigesima seconda'; this latter instrument is almost certainly a small recorder, and a duet in *Orfeo* accompanied by two 'flautini' appears to indicate recorders in C, also used for four bars in the *Vespers* of 1610. Bacon, in his *Natural History*, shows particular interest in which groupings of instruments sound best ('the recorder and stringed music agree well' cent. III § 278), and Morley's *Consort Lessons* (1599) are scored for a fixed consort of treble viol, flute, bass viol, lute, cittern, and pandora, the same consort as is seen in a painting in the National Portrait Gallery playing at the wedding of Sir Henry Unton (d. 1596); this group is also prescribed by Rosseter in his *Lessons for Consort* (1609). By 1619, Praetorius is interested enough in orchestral balance to comment on the weakness in the sonority of the bass in a recorder consort, and it is significant that when Lully uses six recorders in *Psyche* (1671), three of them are basses. As composers became more conscious of tonal effects, so the medieval and Renaissance freedom of instrumentation can be taken advantage of less and less, particularly when the music is composed in a new form, such as the trio-sonata. Purists would not play Purcell's trio-sonatas on two recorders instead of two violins (even though most of them suit the recorder's compass) but they are compensated by having a magnificent chaconne 'three parts upon a ground' in F major (S. Ed. 10340) composed originally for recorders.

Scattered among Purcell's dramatic and vocal works are numerous pieces for 'flutes' (i.e. recorders) which are among the finest things in the recorder's repertoire. The most breath-taking of all is the chaconne in *Dioclesian* (S. Ser. 23), two-part canon written upon a ground bass, but sounding so serene and spontaneous that one is completely unaware of its structural complexity. Three other pieces are collected by Walter Bergmann in S. Ser. 35; they include the symphony introducing the duet for alto and tenor voices 'In vain the am'rous flute' from the *Ode on St. Cecilia's Day* (1692), a work which contains a piece in which two trebles and a bass recorder converse with the strings. Purcell's normal practice, like Bach's, was to use two recorders together, often playing in thirds. Two recorders, bad-tempered and bickering, accompany the soprano song 'Why should men quarrel' (S), in *Theodosius* they accompany the bass voice in 'Hark, behold the heavenly choir', and in the 1694 *Ode on the Birthday of Queen Mary* two recorders combine with contralto voice to 'Strike the Viol' (S). Blow uses two recorders, two counter-tenor voices and thoroughbass in his beautiful *Ode on the Death of Mr. Henry Purcell* (1696), and recorders alternate with strings in his *Venus and Adonis*. One of the few places where the recorder goes untwinned is in the delightful pastoral scene in Purcell's *King Arthur* where recorder and oboe accompany two sopranos in 'Shepherd, shepherd, leave decoying'. With so much excellent music in its repertoire it was not surprising that John Evelyn should write 'The Flute douce [is] now much in request for accompanying the Voice' (*Diary*, 20th November, 1679).

The period 1680–1730 is an age of plenty for English recorder music. Even books of exercises contain music of high merit, such as the piece by Purcell in 'Preludes and Voluntaries' (S) and the Allemande and Fantasia (Nos. 5 and 9) in 'Fifteen Solos' (S). There is more good music in the sonatas for two flutes (i.e. treble recorders) by Finger (Na 561), William Croft (Na 504—Nos. 4 and 5 probably the best: 5 also S. Lib. 8), and Paisible (S: Mk), and Na 507 contains an excellent miscellany of English duets published in 1738 in Amsterdam. J. B. Loeillet's sonatas for recorder and continuo were 'fitted and contrived for 2 flutes' by Walsh the publisher in 1728 (No. 3 in U), and a number of arrangements for the recorder were made of Corelli's works (some trio-sonatas in H), including the famous Follia. Loeillet's sonatas, all of them first-rate music, are published by S (more by DRV and H) who also publish a trio-sonata of his. S have brought out some of Barsanti's sonatas, as well as less exciting works by Pepusch (the composer for *The Beggar's Opera*), Galliard the oboist (also DRV), Valentine (further publications in H), Sammartini and Bononcini, Handel's rival (sonata in U). Two good sonatas and a remarkable set of divisions on a nine-bar ground bass by Henry Purcell's brother Daniel are published by S, OUP, and U respectively, and H publish a

Pepusch trio-sonata for recorder, oboe, and continuo, a pleasant and uncomplicated work. Baston, Babell, and Woodcock are known for their concertos for sixth-flute(s) (descant in D) and strings (S), ingenuous and cheerful works, but in artifice and delicacy excelled by the pastoral cantatas of such writers as Pepusch, Croft, and Arne (S: U), works as English, and as derivative, as Palladian architecture.

Handel's numerous compositions for the flute (as opposed to the 'traversa') are every bit as good as one expects them to be. There are seven sonatas, two trio-sonatas, some occasional pieces (including two pieces in the Water Music scored for 'flauti piccoli'), numerous items in the operas and oratorios, and cantatas including the beautiful 'Nel dolce dell'oblio'. Most of these are published by S, but Mk's edition of four of the sonatas is useful in having the continuo part arranged for strings. An interesting use of the recorder by Handel is in the opera *Rinaldo* where the sopranino, accompanied by two trebles and strings, provided the music for a swarm of sparrows which, according to the disapproving Addison (*Spectator* 5), fluttered around the stage (and auditorium) during (and after) this scene. In *Acis and Galatea* recorders accompany both bass ('O ruddier than the cherry'), and soprano ('Hush ye pretty warbling choir' and 'Heart, the seat of soft delight'). With Handel, as with Purcell, the only way of discovering all he wrote for the recorder is to go through the complete Society edition looking for 'flauto' parts, a long but rewarding task. An excellent article on 'Handel's Use of the Recorder' by Joel Newman of Columbia University is published in Nos. 21 and 22 of *The Recorder News*.

Activity amongst composers in England in writing for the recorder was matched by similar activity in Germany. Schütz and Ahle had used the recorder in their sacred works, and Bach's Cantatas contain some of the greatest music written for the instrument, the noblest of all being Cantata 106, scored for two recorders, two viole da gamba, continuo and voices, 'Gottes Zeit ist die allerbeste Zeit'. Other notable recorder occasions in the Cantatas are the opening choruses of Cantatas 39 and 65, the sonata in

Cantata 182, the concertos in Cantatas 152 and 142, the aria 'Sheep may safely graze' in Cantata 208, and the second recitative in Cantata 161 when, with unforgettable intensity, two recorders and plucked strings strike the hour of death. Recorders are also scored for in Cantatas 13, 18, 25, 46, 71, 81, 96, 103, 119, 122, 127, 175, 180, and 189 (MR, etc.), as well as in the 'Esurientes' of one version of the Magnificat (S), the aria for tenor voice 'O Schmerz' with two recorders and two hautbois de chasse in the St. Matthew Passion (No. 25), and the tenor aria 'Sanfte soll' in the Easter Oratorio (No. 7). Bach uses two recorders in his Fourth Brandenburg Concerto in G major (H: Br & H) and in the F major version of it with solo harpsichord replacing solo violin (Br & H: Cor 32): one recorder combines with trumpet and oboe in the Second Brandenburg Concerto (H: Br & H). Like Telemann, Bach exploits the recorder's high register when there is any danger of it being drowned by other instruments.

Telemann has almost been appropriated by recorder players as their own private composer, so much and so well did he write for the instrument. Although his sonatas (S, Ba, H, and Arnold), especially the pair from 'Essercizii Musici' in D minor and C major (H), are typically melodious and polished, Telemann's most gratifying recorder music is in his trio-sonatas, of which about twenty are obtainable in modern editions (S, Ba, Mk, H, Br & H, Na). The best four are those in A minor for recorder and violin (H), in C minor for recorder and oboe (H) with a most mellifluous third movement, in F major for recorder and viola da gamba (viola or cello) (N. Arch 131), and in B flat for recorder, harpsichord, and thorough-bass (HM 36). Telemann's quartet music, and his greatest music is in this medium, usually calls for transverse flute and not recorder: in one long and wonderful quartet from the *Tafelmusik*, however, he uses one treble recorder, two transverse flutes, and continuo (Br & H). There are also available three other quartets in which recorder and continuo join with violins and viola (M), two violins (S), and violin and oboe (S: H). Among the orchestral work in modern editions there are two good concerti grossi for two

treble recorders and strings (N. Arch 167 and Cor 21), a
virtuoso concerto (HM 130), two suites, one easy (N. Arch
177) and one difficult (H), and a concerto for recorder,
flute, and strings (HM 124). There is an abundance of
cantatas with recorder obbligati, the most delightful being
'Locke Nur' (S). The *Kleine Kammermusik* (HM 47) provides a descant player with six attractive partitas, and
the duets for two treble recorders, including the six
canon-sonatas, (all S) are marvels of taste and invention.

Mattheson's duet-sonatas (S: Na) are tame beside
Telemann's but the respect in which this composer was
held can be better understood from the trios for three treble
recorders (S: Na). Graupner's concerto (S) and Fasch's
two quartet-sonatas (HM 26 and Mk 40) show real understanding of the recorder. One of the latter provides
another example of partnership between recorder and flute,
a combination also used by Loeillet in a quintet for two
flutes, two recorders, and continuo (HM 133) and by
Quantz, Frederick the Great's flute master, in a trio-sonata
(HM 60: another, with violin, in S). German composers
provide some of the curiosities of the recorder's repertoire;
Schickhardt wrote concertos for four recorders and continuo
(Ba), and Heinichen for four recorders, strings, and continuo, and, in a slightly earlier period, Schmeltzer wrote an
ingenious Sonata for seven recorders, usually paired with
Bertali's Sonatella for five recorders (both S). Earlier still
(1620) an anonymous composer of Breslau wrote a 'Sonada
â 3 fiauti & B.C.' (S). Other attractive works in this early
baroque style are Funccius's four-part suites (1677)
(S. Arch 15), Biber's 'Sonata pro Tabula' for five recorders
and five strings, and Rosenmüller's 'sonate da camera' (1670)
(ZfS 114) which, in a good old-fashioned way, call for
'cinque stromenti da arco, et altri' (for Rosenmüller, see
also N. Arch 30).

In France a great deal of music, much of it of merit
though requiring a knowledge of ornamentation to perform
it well, was being written under the general formula
'à musettes, vielles, flûtes à bec, flûtes traversières ou
violons'. Composers of such music were Marin Marais,
Michel de la Barre, and de Caix d'Hervelois, who wrote

mainly to a basso continuo, and Naudot, Aubert, Philibert de la Vigne, Boismortier, and the Chédevilles, who wrote duets without bass. The best introduction to this duet music is the Na 517 publication which contains two superlative Boismortier suites, and the de la Vigne suites published by DRV, beautiful and simple music. There are more duets in Na 26 and HM 81 (Chédeville), and HM 85 and OUP (Boismortier), while S publish Suites compiled from accompanied duets by Marais (also U) and la Barre, as well as a Caix d'Hervelois solo suite which has an invigorating movement called 'Tubœuf'. Boosey publish a Sonata for three flutes by Boismortier, as well as some Couperin arrangements (more in OUP), and DRV publish an admirable concerto by Boismortier for treble recorder, violin, oboe, bassoon, and basso continuo. Couperin's two charming nightingale pieces (U: S) have been made well known by Carl Dolmetsch's performances of them on the sopranino recorder.

The instrumental compositions of Alessandro Scarlatti are small in number, but excellent in quality, and in eighteen of them there are parts for recorders. This music is ideal for the mixed group of recorders and strings as every part is full of interest: the centre-piece of each symphony is a vigorous fugue, but in the outside movements massive chordal writing alternates with polyphony. So far published are five of the twelve symphonies—Nos. 1 and 3 by S, Nos. 4 and 5 in HM (48 and 116), and No. 2, scored for recorder, trumpet, and strings (HM 146), as well as two sonatas for recorder, two violins, and continuo (H and Mk)—one the most engaging, the other the noblest of all the published works, a serene sonata in A major for two recorders, two violins, and continuo (Mk), and a closely interwoven sonata for three recorders and continuo (H: Mk). One wonders how many of Scarlatti's six hundred cantatas, praised for their adventurous harmonies, have recorder parts. Vivaldi's instrumental output was considerably greater than Scarlatti's and scores are available in the complete Ricordi edition. Vivaldi was careful, like Handel, to distinguish between flute and recorder, and occasions when plain 'flauto' is indicated are happily frequent. Two of the best concertos are those for flute, two violins, and continuo (F. XII, No. 11), and for flute, violin, bassoon, and continuo (F. XII, No. 21), and there is a rollicking Allegro on a ground bass as the last movement of the Concerto for flute, oboe, violin, bassoon, and continuo (F. XII, No. 30). Of smaller works the Trio for flute, oboe, and bassoon (F. XII, No. 4: Mk 47), and the Sonata in G minor for recorder and continuo from 'Il Pastor Fido' (HM 135:S) are outstanding. Excellent recorder sonatas were also composed by Benedetto Marcello (OUP: HM 142, 151–2) and Francesco Veracini (Rudall Carte).

The eighteenth century

From the middle of the eighteenth century onwards music composed for recorders becomes almost non-existent. Interesting exceptions are that swan-song of the recorder, the 'Dance of the Blessed Spirits' in Gluck's *Orfeo* (1761) (S)—a final proof of the association of the instrument with another world, and the obbligato to Rosine's aria in Paisiello's *Le Barbier de Séville* (1785) 'Rien ne peut calmer ma peine' (S). The recorder player will find that for private consumption—that is, not for public performance—much of the music written for the flute in the eighteenth century fits his instrument without difficulty. Indeed he may argue in excusing such piracy that the tone of the modern flute differs from the tone of the eighteenth-century flute as much as does the recorder, and that composers up to the time of Mozart thought of recorders as an alternative (even if only to extend their sales) when writing for the flute, for recorders were being made, and presumably played upon, until the beginning of the nineteenth century. In this way the recorder's repertoire is considerably extended. There are six Bach flute sonatas (recorder transpositions in S, H.D 706 and Mitteldeutscher Verlag—MR), a solo Bach sonata (H: ed. U), parts of the Suite in B minor (S), and four trio-sonatas (H), including the greatest of all trio-sonatas, that from the *Musical Offering*. More than one arranger has tried his hand with *The Art of Fugue* which, with its clear four-part writing, sounds surprisingly effective as a recorder consort, and some of the choral preludes respond well to the same treatment (S—'Bibliothek' series: OUP). The three hundred and seventy-one chorales (Br & H: Nov) are admirable material for the consort, and a trio of tenor recorder, viola, and cello whose technique is good may lay claim to the five trios and six 'organ' trio-sonatas (H: Nov), the last two of which are as exciting as the Brandenburg concertos.

The only recorder work written by the sons of Bach is the trio for viola, bass recorder, and keyboard by C. P. E. Bach (1775) (S), but many of their chamber works intended for flute(s) may be played (in camera) on the recorder, notably C. P. E. Bach's Trio-Sonata in B flat (H 4237) and twelve short pieces for two flutes, some with keyboard (Zimmermann), and **W**. F. Bach's Trio-Sonata in F major (H 6042) and six duet sonatas (Br & H). J. C. Bach—the 'London Bach'—wrote some charming quartets and quintets which go well with recorder substituted for flute (HM 119, H.D162, HM 42, N. Arch 123 and 124, and S. Ed. 5548), and the same may be said for his friend and admirer Mozart's flute quartets, although the fourth in A major has to be treated in a Procrustean fashion to make it fit. Much of Mozart's simpler music admits of arrangement for the recorder (e.g. H.P 4555). The 'Drei Leichte Trios' published by H (CO 707) for flute, violin, and cello are a 'natural' for the treble recorder. The Haydn Baryton trios (HM 65, 94, 95) are playable on the descant recorder, but the six trios op. 100 (Zimmermann) are much more rewarding, for this great music suits the treble recorder's tone-quality and compass ideally. Of the Trio in F published by S, the editor (Walter Bergmann) writes, 'The flute part is so well written for the treble recorder that one is inclined to think that the composer or arranger had this instrument, at least as another possibility, in mind'. The London trios (N. Arch 71) sound well on treble, violin or tenor, and cello. Less comfortable Haydn flute pieces are the Quartet in G (N. Arch 129), the Quintet in D (H.D68), the three trios for flute, cello, and clavier (Br & H), and the flute-clock music (Na 538). James Hook is another composer whose flute music is much pirated by recorder players (sonatas and duets by S, trios by S and Boos.), but Stamitz has been surprisingly neglected, even though his duets

(N. Arch 62 and 178), a trio (HM 106) and an eloquent quartet (HM 109) are 'apt for recorders'. Blavet's duets (DRV) are equally suitable. Quartets by William Shield, Abel (both S), and Wendling (N. Arch 191), flute trio-sonatas by Quantz and others, Telemann's flute solos, duets (Ba), and quartets (two by Zimmermann, N. Arch 24 and Br & H), de Fesch's sonatas (U), duets (S) and trio-sonatas (H 6041), Roman's sonatas (HM 101, and four arranged for treble in H.D847–8), Boccherini's flute quintets (MR), and a 'Concerto a 4' by Handel (S. Ant) can all enter the recorder's repertoire with only the slightest infringement of authenticity.

It appears to have been the occasional practice in the early eighteenth-century orchestra for oboes to be inter-changeable with recorders, especially in slow movements. Indeed in such works as Handel's concertos (op. 3) pub-lishers, at least, offer a choice of woodwind instruments (recorders are actually stipulated in the slow movement of op. 3, No. 1). It is an historically correct expedient, there-fore, to substitute recorders for oboes in the symphonic works of the early eighteenth century. A group of strings and recorders may reasonably explore the overtures and symphonies of Boyce and others in the Oxford Orchestral Series, particularly Nos. 62–4, 69, 116–17, and 123 (Boyce), 31 and 128 (Handel), and 119 (Arne), and in the Augener series of early classical works, particularly Handel—Overture *Esther*, J. C. Bach—Symphony in B♭, and Filtz—Symphony in E♭).

Appropriations from other sources

A recorder player knowing the practices of various periods can find suitable music from a wide variety of sources. Country dance music, for example, is a legitimate hunting-ground for arrangers. Thoinot Arbeau in the treatise on dancing *Orchésographie* (1588), mentions that the recorder is useful in accompanying dances, and Henry Playford writes (1691) that 'the *Treble Violin* and *Flute* are . . . the delight of most Young Practitioners in *Musick* for their Chearful and Sprightly sounds in setting forth the . . . Newest *Tunes*, *Ayres*, *Jiggs* and *Minuets* . . . in Use at

Publick Theatres and at Dancing Schools'. There is good authority, therefore, for such recorder arrangements as Freda Dinn's sixteenth-century dances (S. Arch 1 and 2), Meech's Playford trios (S), and Bergmann's brilliant 'Apted Book' dances (S). Playford's remarks may also be made the excuse for playing Purcell's dramatic music (Nov, Augener, HM 50 and 58) with strings and recorders mixed. Early baroque music which might primarily have been intended for other instruments may, according to the practice of the period, be transferred to recorders. Some early trio-sonatas such as Salomone Rossi's 'detta La Moderna' (HM 110: for more Rossi see S. Ed 4096) sound surprisingly well with a recorder in the upper part, and Frescobaldi's *Canzoni per Sonar* (S. Ant), which were possibly meant for violins or cornetts (although 'accommodate per sonar con ogni sorte di stromenti'), suit tenor recorders and bass, or a mixed ensemble. In some cantatas of the period (e.g. Buxtehude's setting of 'In Dulci Jubilo' (Ba)) obbligati parts for two or three violins can be 'accommodated' to recorders. There is much excellent music to be found in the repertoire of the 'Royal Wind Music', which included recorder-players from 1540 onwards; selections are published by OUP, including a noble suite in five parts by Locke. At a later date, Purcell's Chacony for three high instruments and a bass (S. Ant) makes a valuable addition to the recorder's repertoire. Adventurous recorder players will appropriate any good chamber music in which the instrumentation is indefinite.

Arrangements of music specifically composed for other instruments are valid provided that no pretence is made that they are original recorder music, and that they suit the instrument. In this, good taste must be the judge. John Stanley's organ voluntaries (OUP), Peter Warlock's *Capriol Suite* (Boos.), or even the Madrigal from *The Mikado* (Joseph Williams) are appropriate to arrange for a recorder consort: Tchaikovsky's Andante Cantabile (S) is not.

The twentieth century

The first appearance of the recorder in modern music in this country after its nineteenth-century hibernation is said to be in Robin Milford's oratorio, *A Prophet in the Land* (1930), and since then, spurred on by commissions such as those of Carl Dolmetsch for his annual Wigmore Hall concerts and of Manuel Jacobs in the late thirties, composers have written for the recorder with increasing understanding of its capabilities. Some of the best works are for recorder and keyboard, the outstanding compositions being Lennox Berkeley's Sonatina (S), Edmund Rubbra's 'Meditazione sulla Cœurs Désolés' (Lengnick) suitably melancholy and archaic, Herbert Murrill's Sonata (OUP) which, like Antony Hopkins' joyful Suite (S), uses the four-movement form of a Handel sonata, Franz Reizenstein's vigorous Partita (S), Cyril Scott's lush 'Aubade' (S), and Martin Shaw's difficult and serious Sonata in E flat (Cramer). There are good things in Walter Leigh's elegiac Sonatina (S), Norman Fulton's Scottish Suite (S), Malcolm Arnold's Sonatina (Paterson), and Stanley Bate's Sonatina (S), the last movement of which is music of a machine age.

Amongst the best music by modern British composers for recorder consort are two four-part pieces originally intended for bamboo pipes, Vaughan Williams's Suite (OUP), and Rubbra's Air and Variations (Lengnick). Racine Fricker's Trio (S), and Michael Tippett's four short duets (S), both commissioned by the Society of Recorder Players, are satisfying works; in a less serious vein Benjamin Britten's Scherzo for quartet and Alpine Suite for trio (both Boos.), Francis Baines's brassy and invigorating Fantasia for three descant and three treble recorders (S), and Timothy Moore's Suite for trio (S) might be picked out of a wide but not particularly distinguished field. Music composed for recorder and strings is still as yet small in volume but its quality is impressive. Rubbra's 'Fantasia on a Theme of Machaut' (Lengnick), Gordon Jacob's seven-movement Suite (OUP), Arnold Cooke's Concerto (S), and Arthur Milner's 'Eclogue' (H) are all works that both please at first hearing and reward study.[1]

An enormous quantity of recorder music has emanated

[1] Robert Simpson's Variations and Fugue for recorder and string quartet was highly praised at its first performance in February 1959—too late for inclusion in this survey.

from Germany but much of it is lacking in inspiration, despite the high standard set by Hindemith in his trio (1932—S), particularly in its moving Fugato. Compositions by Staeps (sonata—U, duets—S, Flötentänze quartets—Haslinger/S), Burghardt (one sonata and two trio-sonatas—Ba), Genzmer (sonata, trio, and quartet—S), Müller-Hartmann (trio—S), Koerppen (one vast sonata—Br & H), Jentsch ('Four Emblems'—MR), and Wischer (Kleine Dorischer Suite—H.D 251) all deserve mention, the latter if only for a remarkably brash four-part fugue.

Lerich's pleasant Trio for recorder, violin, and viola (H.D834) is one of the few modern pieces that are easy without being drab; a besetting sin of twentieth-century music is that it is seldom both simple and serious. Good attempts at compromise are made by Armin Knab in his Pastorale and Allegro for two recorders and guitar (Ba), Robin Milford in his Sonatina, Christmas Pastoral, and Three Pieces (all OUP), Benjamin Burrows in his Suite (S), and Antony Hopkins in his Four Dances, which have the added interest of marking the return of the recorder to the London stage, for they were specially composed for an Arts Theatre Club production of Shaw's *Back to Methuselah* in 1946. Since then the recorder has consolidated its dramatic connections by featuring in a musical comedy on the life of Pepys, *And So To Bed* (1951—music by Vivian Ellis), and in a children's opera by Britten, *Noyes Fludde* (1958). Relatively little has been composed during this century for recorders in the rôle in which they once excelled—to accompany the voice, although Rubbra ('Cantata Pastorale'—Lengnick), Tippett (S), Zillah Castle (S), and a few others have experimented in this medium. After so many centuries of recorder music Bacon's words (*Natural History*, cent. III § 278) still hold good—'for the melioration of music there is yet much left, in this point of exquisite consorts, to try and inquire'.

Details of some recorder publications issued since the first impression of this book, will be found on p. 141.

III

KINDS OF RECORDERS:
CHOOSING AN INSTRUMENT

Description

A recorder is basically an open tube blown at one end in which sound is produced by the impinging of the air-stream shaped by a windway upon an edge formed by the chamfering of the surface of the tube. This principle of sound formation is used for the flute, the only difference being that a flute-player shapes the air-stream with his lips. A page of this book can be made to produce a convincing edge-tone: hold the book open with both hands so that one page is separated and bring the edge of the page to about a quarter of an inch from the lips, keeping the page in a horizontal position. Now blow softly a very thin stream of air directly on to the edge, and, with adjustment, a quiet wavering squeak will result. This squeak is caused by the formation of eddies on each side of the page which produce regular alternations of pressure and set the air around vibrating (for further details and diagrams consult books such as *Music and Sound* by Ll. S. Lloyd, London, 1951). In the flute and the recorder these vibrations are modified by being 'coupled' to a tube the sounding length of which may be altered by opening and closing holes in it with the fingers and thumb. The recorder uses eight such holes, although the two lower holes should be doubled to facilitate the production of semitones.

Further experiment with the edge of the page, blowing even more softly and holding the page a little farther from the mouth, will produce a very quiet edge-tone of low enough pitch to be identified on the piano: this illustrates the principle that the softer one blows the lower the note, and vice versa. This principle is used to obtain high notes on the flageolet (which normally has six finger-holes), and on the tabor-pipe, which, with its long, narrow bore susceptible to harmonics, can produce two octaves from three holes by the use of different breath-pressures of over-blowing. Unless the cross-sectional area of the windway can be controlled (as in the lips of the flute-player), over-blowing means more air, and more air creates more sound, so on the flageolet the upper octave must needs be louder than the lower. The formation of harmonics on a wind instrument can, however, be achieved without any increase of breath-pressure by opening a small hole (octave-hole or 'speaker') between the source of vibration and the first open finger-hole: on the recorder this is usually done by partially opening the thumb-hole (see p. 49). The superi-ority of the recorder over other end-blown flutes lies in its ability to play notes of the upper octave more softly than those of the lower octave.

The windway of a recorder is formed by the insertion of an incised plug or block (whence the German name 'Blockflöte') into the blown end of the tube, which is generally made beak-shaped (whence 'Flûte à bec') to fit between the lips. This block is made of a wood such as red cedar which does not swell with moistening. The opening of the windway opposite the edge is chamfered slightly to direct the air in the best way against the edge: this process is called 'voicing'. The edge itself is the most delicate part of a recorder and should not be touched. It should be straight, smooth, and clean. There is some doubt as to whether the title 'fipple' should be accorded to the plug or to the edge: as the edge is the most distinctive feature of the 'fipple-flute' family it seems likely to be that, but Francis Bacon confused the issue by defining fipple as 'the plug at the mouth of a wind-instrument, by which its volume was contracted', a definition copied in the Oxford English Dictionary. The word derives from 'flipi', meaning 'lip', and is said to be still in use in the Northumbrian dialect where to 'hang the fipple' is to let the lower lip drop, or to look dejected.

Recorders are usually made in three parts, the upper part being called the head, and the lower the foot. The head should be aligned to the body of the instrument so that the holes are straight with the centre of the windway; the foot should be turned so that the holes can be covered by the fleshy part of the little finger in an unbent position. When the best position of the foot has been established by practice and experience, marks should be made on each side of the joint so that this position can be returned to every time the instrument is assembled. The joints are lapped with cork, rubber or waxed thread, and are protected from cracking by bulges of wood, ivory rings or metal straps. All recorders bigger than a descant should have a thumb-rest. It should be in such a position that the right hand is made to lie roughly at right-angles to the instrument (see p. 47). Cork-faced rests, if not supplied with the instrument, can be obtained from an instrument dealer and fixed with the small screws supplied and or with glue. Some players prefer to use thumb-hooks: they give good support, but can be uncomfortable and look ugly.

Recorder tone

Although the recorder has a tone-quality of its own which is distinguishable from that of any other woodwind instrument, save perhaps a flute played by a master, there is considerable variation between one instrument and another. As with sherries, certain characteristics become associated with different makers: the tone-quality of every recorder, therefore, is something that has been deliberately aimed at by the maker, and not a matter of chance.

A recorder's tone is affected by three things, its voicing, its bore, and the material it is made of. Of these the most important is voicing, and it is in the skill and understanding with which the craftsman matches the voicing to the nature of the piece of wood he is working with, and to its future maturing as a musical instrument, that the hand-made wood recorder is so superior to a machine-made instrument, although misjudgement or bad luck could result in a hand-made recorder being a very poor thing. The most critical factor in voicing is in the way the edge divides the air into two parts, one vibrating in the bore, the other escaping along the top of the instrument. An uneven division of air favours the tone of the lower notes of the instrument, and minimizes differences in quality between the notes of this register (e.g. between F, a weak note, and G, a robust note), but this voicing makes it difficult to get good high notes, which are better produced with an equal parting of the air-stream. The distance between the opening of the windway and the edge is also a factor in tone production, the higher register being favoured by closeness, although too close a voicing stifles the tone: if this distance is made greater the lower notes are favoured, although too great a distance means that less air is made to sound, so causing fluffiness. The cross-sectional areas of the windway and of the bore affect tone because they determine the amount of breath needed to make a note. A greater distance between the roof and floor of the windway favours the lower notes as more vibrating air can be expended on them, but in a fatter instrument what is gained in loudness is lost in expense of breath and a resultant lack of control of phrasing, particularly in the higher register. The precise shape of the cross-sectional area of the windway, which is sometimes straight across and sometimes an arc shape, has no effect on tone, but the slightest impedance to the progress of the breath travelling through the windway causes fluffiness and makes it harder to obtain high notes. If the height of the walls on either side of the edge is great a reedy and 'edgy' tone results, while purer and more 'open' tones emerge when the 'window' of the recorder is shallow.

The historical development of the shape of the recorder bore makes an interesting study in taste. The instruments illustrated by Virdung (1511) were fat and almost cylindrical, and must have sounded loud and clear but a trifle monotonous. Their tone would be pure but would have no 'bite' to it: their range was probably little more than an octave, for with a wide bore it is difficult to get the clear round harmonics that make the second octave of the recorder. The recorder as it was used in *Hamlet* (1604) was considerably narrower though still made in one piece: it had taken on a more conical shape with a slight flare at the foot. It would certainly have played two full octaves and its tone would be pure, round, and rather dispassionate and abstract—in fact ideal for most Elizabethan consort music. The baroque instrument, such as is in general use today, has a much more conical bore and therefore an impure, reedy, and more penetrating sound, bearing the same relationship to its Elizabethan ancestor as the violin to the viol. The shaping of the conical bore would have been facilitated in the baroque era by the instrument being no longer made in one piece; the bulges and rings of the baroque instrument, though a practical necessity, delightfully reflect the decorative taste of the time.

The third factor influencing tone is the material of which the instrument is made: as Bacon puts it, 'When the sound is created between the blast of the mouth and the air of the pipe, it hath nevertheless some communication with the matter of the sides of the pipe, and the spirits in them contained' (*Natural History*, cent. II § 167). Wood is undoubtedly the most satisfactory material for making recorders. Bacon suggested that 'it were good to try recorders and hunters' horns of brass, what the sound would be', (cent. III § 234). The effect would not be pleasant as brass has a ringing tone of its own which would react favourably to some notes and unfavourably to others, resulting in inequality and hardness. The same is true, to a more limited extent, with plastics such as Bakelite and with hard living tissues such as ebony-wood and ivory, although some beautiful-looking recorders of carved ivory are preserved in museums. The best wood for recorders has no knots and a close and parallel grain that allows a surface to be made which stays smooth even under conditions of frequent wetting and drying, without splintering or swelling. It should not be so hard that it has too violent a resonance of its own, nor so soft that it absorbs or dampens sound. The woods that most nearly meet these requirements are box, rosewood, tulip-wood, satin-wood, beef-wood, cocobolo, jacaranda, palisander, granadilla, olive, and African blackwood.[1] Slightly softer woods such as maple, pear, cherry, walnut, and beech are also suitable for recorder making, especially if they are made impermeable to moisture by heat treatment followed by impregnation with paraffin wax, but although such impregnated instruments if well made produce a delicate and silvery

[1] Hildemarie Peter, in her book on the recorder (see p. 61), provides a chart giving the specific gravity and modulus of elasticity of these woods.

sound, they are somehow less satisfying to play upon than naturally seasoned wood with its greater individuality and vitality. Although one may have a *penchant* towards, say, box or rosewood, it is said that the hardwoods listed above do not each produce a characteristic tone-quality: the differences in tone between instruments made by the same maker depend more on the subtle relationship between voicing and the nature of the piece of wood used for each instrument.

Care of the recorder

First and foremost, keep your recorder in a stout wooden box that shuts firmly. Any container that does not protect the recorder when it is dropped is useless. Never leave a recorder on the floor or on a chair or perched on a music stand. Do not let a recorder get hot: heat dries out natural wood and makes a recorder made of impregnated wood sweat drops of paraffin wax.

After playing wipe the recorder bore dry with a mop or piece of material that does not shed fluff. Do not force a mop into a recorder nor push it into the head-piece up against the plug. The best recorder wiper is probably a linen handkerchief rolled diagonally and twisted gently through the bore of the instrument: it leaves no bits, dries moisture, and polishes the surface of the bore. About once a quarter it is wise to oil the bore of a recorder other than one made of impregnated wood with a non-softening, non-acid, resinating plant oil such as banana, almond or unboiled linseed (not olive): these oils leave a thin protecting film on the surface of the bore. If too much oil is used it dries sticky and attracts fluff, as well as deadening the benign influence of the wood-spirits. The outside of a recorder is usually varnished, so oil cannot affect it either beneficially or adversely, although an old recorder with the varnish worn off does benefit from occasional oiling, and a new one looks smarter. On no account let oil touch the tone-producing regions which must remain as pervious to moisture as possible: oil on the edge and thereabouts encourages the formation of globules, those recorder player's 'gremlins'. It is best, too, to keep oil away from the plug which might be loosened by lubrication. When applying oil, warm it in the palm of the hand first so that it becomes thinner and penetrates the surface of the wood before drying.

Joints should be airtight, and should be snug enough not to allow 'play' in the lower sections of the instrument, particularly the foot. Instruments should be assembled and taken to pieces by screwing firmly and gently in the direction of the lapping of the joint (clockwise), without any sideways force. If cork joints are loose they may be made to swell slightly with moistening, or can be burred with a pin: another method is to grease the cork and then warm it lightly over a match flame. Thread joints can be varied at will by winding off or adding thread; bobbins of soft and resilient waxed thread are obtainable from wood-wind suppliers, or cobbler's hemp rubbed with beeswax or soaked in melted candle-wax may be used. If the inner section of a joint cracks it should be bound tightly between the lapping and the bottom of the joint with fine and inelastic wire such as five-amp. fuse-wire. A crack on the outer sleeve of a joint is more disturbing and the instrument should at once be returned to the maker to be fitted with a retaining ring. If a cork joint becomes so worn that a section of the instrument is loose this too is a case for hospital treatment with the maker, not just first-aid with pieces of thin paper. Cork joints can be preserved by applying lanolin, enough of which can be obtained for a few pence from a chemist to last the recorder's life-time. Lanolin also makes a stiff cork joint easier to operate and it is a good idea to put some on the joints of brand-new instruments before assembling them. Soap, tallow or Vaseline have the same effect..

After a certain amount of use the thumb-hole of a wooden instrument wears away with the rubbing of the thumb-nail on it. Experienced players do not 'thumb' violently so they are less troubled with this disorder. With a badly worn thumb-hole it is difficult to judge the width of the space left between the thumb-nail and the edge of the instrument ('thumbing aperture') and high notes are there-fore hard to form. The instrument-maker should then be asked to 're-bush' the thumb-hole, preferably with ivory.

To keep the windway free of fluff and deposit, it should be wiped out with a feather, taking care not to let the feather push against the edge. Accumulated deposit at the corners of the windway and the edge should be eased off with a cardboard matchstick and infinite care. Before a performance, a feather dipped in a weak detergent solution may be passed through the windway to remove patches of grease which attract moisture, and immediately afterwards the windway should be washed through thoroughly with a little warm water so that no detergent whatsoever remains that might damage the wood : shake out as much water as possible from the windway, wipe the outside of the instrument and allow it to dry.

New wooden recorders need playing-in to break the wood gently to its task of maintaining its personality under varying conditions of temperature and humidity. However tempting it might be to go on, a player with a new instrument should stop playing after half an hour for the first week or so of the recorder's life, and dry the instrument thoroughly before putting it away. A month-old recorder will last out a normal playing session without danger of the wood cracking. With proper care, however, its tone will continue to improve as it adapts itself to its owner and as the owner comes to recognize its qualities and idiosyncrasies.

Sizes of recorders

Although Praetorius lists eight sizes of recorders, nowadays only six are in use, three in C and three in F.

The most important member of the family is the treble in F, (German 'altblockflöte'). It has neither the shrillness of the smaller instruments nor the lack of prominence of tone-quality of the bigger recorders. In the early eighteenth century the treble recorder was known simply as 'flute', and for it were written the major baroque works in which a recorder is featured—the Second Brandenburg Concerto or Handel's 'flauto' sonatas, for example. Accordingly this book is compiled in terms of the treble recorder. Intending players who hope to play sonatas and chamber works with other instruments should start on the treble, rather than approach it, as is so often done, via the descant.

The descant (in C, a fifth above the treble), enjoys a not altogether deserved popularity because of its cheapness and its suitability for use in schools. It is also known as the 'soprano', and, being the nearest modern instrument to the old 'sixth-flute' in D (i.e. a sixth above the standard treble), can claim a small repertoire of eighteenth-century concertos. The most important rôle of the descant, however, is to play the top line, and lead, in consort music. The low breath-pressure required in consort music together with its propensity to 'cry out on the top of question' makes the descant a difficult instrument to manage: its notes are all too often coarse, out of tune and wavering, while high up it can be unbearably shrill. Its importance in consort music and arrangements nevertheless makes its mastery essential: to play it well is a most worth-while achievement.

The sopranino in F, an octave above the treble, is a charming little instrument of limited value. It is referred to as 'flauto piccolo' (e.g. by Handel) or 'ottavino' (by Vivaldi, who wrote three concertos for it) and makes not infrequent appearances to accompany the soprano voice, generally in ornithological contexts. The sopranino has a smaller tone than the descant, but in its higher register it can compete with a sizeable string orchestra. Amongst its small repertoire are a few consort and other arrangements. Sopranino recorders are often made in one part: their bore is so narrow that a pipe-cleaner has to be used for a mop—great care must be taken not to stick the sharp end into the plug. Players with broad finger-tips might have difficulty in fingering a sopranino: for some trills the fingers have to be bunched up most uncomfortably.

The tenor recorder is in C, a fourth below the treble. Because of the big stretch of the little finger, most makers supply a foot with a key to cover the hole. This has the disadvantage that, unless a double key is provided, the note C♯ is missing. Sometimes fingering is made easier by arranging the holes out of line (a sensible device although it mars the beauty of the instrument), or by cutting holes obliquely. A player who intends to specialize in consort music and who cannot afford a bass might well start on the tenor, which is probably the simplest of recorders to play, despite the stretch of its fingering, as good tone-quality is relatively easy to achieve. The tenor's rather subdued tone makes it less suited to solo performance than the treble, and it is altogether overawed by a piano.

The possession of a bass recorder (in F, an octave below the treble) is a passport to popularity amongst recorder players. It is incredible how the addition of a bass recorder to a consort consisting of descants, trebles, and tenors adds richness of sound, moulds good intonation and makes the ensemble more coherent. Even one bass in a numerous consort makes a lot of difference, although its sound is soon engulfed by strings or an accompanying piano. Bass recorders are made either on the bassoon pattern with a crook or on the standard recorder pattern like a tenor but bent in the middle for ease of fingering (e.g. the 'Knick-system' Adler basses). All basses have keys for the lowest note and some have keys as alternatives to wide stretches elsewhere on the instrument. Generally speaking, however, the fewer keys the better; they affect the resonance of the wood, are sometimes noisy in operation, need maintaining, and spoil the simple design of the instrument. Woods used for making basses are usually lighter in weight, such as pearwood or sycamore. Bass recorders use up rather more breath than other recorders so the ability to breath deeply becomes a necessity, and good phrasing is all the more vital. Once the bass clef has been mastered it is not difficult to play a bass recorder adequately but to play it well calls for a deal of musicianship.

Great basses in C, an octave below the tenor, are still uncommon in this country although they are being made regularly by Adler, Moeck, and Stieber in Germany, where they are known as 'gross-bass' recorders. The great bass measures about four and a quarter feet in length and is blown through a long crook: if one plays it sitting down its weight can be taken on the floor by means of an adjustable stand (like a cello's), and if one stands up it can be slung like an F bass. The only fingers to cover holes direct are the middle fingers of each hand, for the remaining holes are operated by means of open-standing keys. The stretch is therefore no greater than it is for a treble. The great bass opens up a wealth of consort music that goes too low for the bass in F. Its tone is bigger than that of the F bass and it gives a booming *fundamento* to a consort. Like the F bass it can be coaxed to play a third octave (see p. 97) although the highest notes are wheezy and uncertain. Its low notes are as profound as could be desired (although sometimes slow in 'speaking'), and it is a shock to be reminded that it goes no lower than a viola. In this instrument the common quality of a recorder note of appearing to sound an octave below its actual pitch (through the absence of prominent upper harmonics) is at its most evident.

Choosing an instrument

As recorders vary so much in tone-quality try as many makes of recorders as possible before choosing. If you are not knowledgeable about recorders persuade a friend who is, to choose for you, for even if you are buying a cheap instrument a pound badly spent can cause a lot of musical frustration. If only one make of instrument is obtainable ask the dealer to get out at least half a dozen as even machine-made plastic instruments vary. Faced with a tableful of instruments test them as follows:

(i) Tone. Play lower C and upper C^I (treble). If the instrument does not give the tone you are looking for (making allowance for your own possible lack of skill in producing good tone), discard it.

(ii) Intonation. Check octaves for intonation. If F to F^I, A to A^I, C to C^I, and D to D^I are in tune, test the scale of F major going down, listening carefully for each interval; bottom F is a note that tends to be out of tune. Next test the sequence C$\sharp$, D$\sharp$, E, F$\sharp^I$, G$\sharp^I$, making sure that the last interval is not too wide.

(iii) Speech. Rapidly repeated staccato C$\sharp$'s will reveal if an instrument is slow in 'speech' (i.e. playing pure note instantaneously upon breath being put into the recorder). Give the instrument a chance by using light tonguing. Try the speed of reaction of notes with forked fingerings such as B$\flat$ and of low notes such as F, as well as of high notes (E^I, F^{II}, G^{II}).

(iv) Volume. Do a rapid crescendo on F, C, and C^1 to see how loud you can get before the note 'breaks'.

(v) Alternative fingerings. See that alternative G^1, E, and D are usable as regards intonation and tone-quality.

(vi) Construction. Check that the instrument has no incipient cracks, that there are no loose splinters of wood round the windway edge and the holes, that the joints are smooth and snug, that the plug is not loose, and that the instrument is well designed and solidly made.

Makes of instruments

A summary of makes of recorders at present available in this country is provided in an appendix to this book (see p. 136).

IV

BEGINNING TO PLAY THE RECORDER

''Tis as easy as lying: govern these ventages with your
fingers and thumb, give it breath with your mouth, and
it will discourse most eloquent music.'

Hamlet, III. ii. 379

A person with an elementary knowledge of the rudiments
of music and a reasonable sense of rhythm should be able
to play the recorder well enough after an hour's practice
every evening for a fortnight to be able to join competently
in consort playing. This chapter describes the process from
the beginning to this stage: the remaining chapters introduce the player to problems of technique that must be
mastered if he is going to lead a consort or to play solo
sonatas or chamber-music with other instruments. Instruction is given in terms of the main member of the recorder
family, the treble recorder. Fingerings are indicated by
figures in three groups: 0 for the left thumb, 1, 2, and 3 for
the first three fingers of the left hand, and 4, 5, 6, and 7 for
the fingers of the right hand: thus a fingering with all holes
covered is represented 0 123 4567. A diagonal line
through a number indicates that the corresponding hole is
half covered, an asterisk denotes a trilling finger.

A player with no previous knowledge of music will need
to obtain a tutor, such as Freda Dinn's *A Systematic Method
for Treble Recorder* (Schott), in which some instruction in
notation is provided, or alternatively to use one of the
many school recorder tutors, most of which are written in
terms of the descant recorder (a cheaper proposition for
Education Authorities). Of school recorder tutors Robert
Noble, writing in *Making Music* (the journal of the Rural
Music Schools Association) in autumn 1956, asked, 'Is
there anywhere else in the whole field of educational
publishing a literature so remarkable for its inadequacies
and inconsistencies?' This serves as a warning to use
only recently published tutors written or sponsored by

experienced recorder teachers and performers such as Carl
Dolmetsch, Edgar Hunt, or Walter Bergmann.

In the early stages it is essential to have books of tunes
and easy pieces to play. Here again the descant player is
better catered for (e.g. *The Oxford Books of Recorder Pieces*,
OUP), but some books of tunes for the treble recorder are
now appearing in catalogues of recorder music (e.g. Schott
editions 10492/3 and 4248A) and there is further material
in recorder tutors, notably in F. J. Giesbert's *Method for
the Recorder in F* (Schott) (the text of this work is misleading
and should be ignored, see p. 90).

The recorder is normally played with the left hand
uppermost (i.e. nearer the head) and the right hand
covering the lower finger-holes. Non-conformists who
prefer to play the other way round, however, are at no
particular disadvantage (other than perhaps having to have
slanting double-holes tailor-made), and can claim good
precedent as the youngest of the three recorder players in
the consort pictured in Ganassi's *Fontegara* (1535) is
playing right hand up without apparently provoking the
disapproval of his elders. Many old instruments catered
for this by providing two little finger-holes at the bottom of
the recorder, the unwanted one being filled with wax,
whence the name 'flûte à neuf trous'.

Take up the recorder, then, with the left hand, placing
the thumb firmly over the underneath hole, and the first
finger firmly on the uppermost finger-hole. The right
thumb should be brought up to the thumb-rest to give
support, and the recorder should, for the moment, be held
with the mouthpiece resting on the chin. The recorder
should make an angle to the floor exactly half-way between
horizontal and perpendicular. If the elbows are kept
comfortably in (as if sitting at table for a meal) and the
wrists below the level of the instrument so that a straight
line from fingertip to elbow passes through the centre of
the wrist, the part of the finger covering the hole should be
the pad, its fleshiest part, and not the tip; the line of the
fingers should be roughly at right-angles to the recorder.
In this position the thumb-hole has to be covered not with

the centre of the thumb's pad, but at a point well to the left (facing the thumb-nail) off-centre and right up against the thumb-nail itself—in fact if it is not cut short enough the thumb-nail will actually touch the instrument. To check the position squeeze the recorder hard between the thumb and forefinger and look at the impression made on the flesh. The circle on the thumb should be no more than an eighth of an inch from the thumb-nail and entirely within the left-hand side of the thumb: that on the fore-finger should be at least a quarter of an inch away from the finger-tip and slightly offset to the left of the finger-pad. Now, having got the thumb and first-finger holes tightly covered, begin groping around with the pad of the second finger for the second hole down. Feel right round its edges, and when its location is certain press the finger home so that the edges make an impression on the flesh. Next lift the finger just off the hole and pat the hole gently and slowly three or four times in the manner of a golfer about to drive a ball. Now hit the hole harder, taking the finger farther off between each stroke, and finally subject the hole to a storm of hammer-blows. Each blow should cause a percussive musical note to sound. It is the note D: check on the piano. The hole's imprint on the finger should be dead central and nearly half an inch from the finger-tip. Hold the second finger tight down and look at its position. The main finger-joint should be bent through about forty-five degrees, and should be on the same level as the finger-nails: the upper finger-joint should be slightly bent. Look in a mirror to make sure that the line of this finger makes an exact right-angle to the line of the recorder. Turn sideways to the mirror and look to see that the line down the finger, across the back of the hand, through the centre of the wrist and up the arm to the elbow is straight.

Still holding on as hard as possible, deliver hammer-blows with the third finger on to its hole, having established its location by groping, pressing, and patting. This should produce a percussive C. The little finger of the left hand, incidentally, will probably be flying around in a most uncontrolled manner during this operation, but that is no matter as it takes little part in recorder playing. This 'grope, press, pat, and hammer' method is the quickest and best way of learning to finger the recorder, and should be applied as each new note is learnt. In the early stages of recorder playing the fingers should grip the instrument so that the complete circumference of the hole beneath them can be felt: as a player gains experience the pads of his fingers become more sensitive and he can feel each hole with the lightest of touches.

The time has now come to start playing. Go back to the thumb and forefinger hold, grip it tight to make sure it is perfect and lift the recorder to the lower lip as if it were a wine-glass you were about to drink from. Relax your fingering for a moment to feel the balance of the instrument, held lightly between the lower lip and the right hand's thumb-rest. Now bring down the upper lip to close the mouth round the mouth-piece, and push your tongue forward into the wind-channel: this last move ensures that the teeth are far enough apart to allow an unimpeded flow of breath. Bring the tongue back and find that place on the roof of the mouth immediately behind the front teeth where a slight abutment is formed (the 'teeth-ridge'). Let the upper part of the tip of the tongue touch this ridge very delicately, then, without vocalising any sound, whisper into the recorder a syllable that, if spoken aloud, would be represented as 'dhoo' (see p. 59). The 'd' sound should be very soft indeed, no common English spluttering 'd', but fearful and unobtrusive.

The result will probably be thoroughly disappointing. It will be a musical note (which is more than first attempts produce on other wind instruments), but, even if the spluttering is avoided, it will probably be harsh and uneven. Consider, therefore, how much air is being put into the instrument. It needs no more than is used for reading aloud or soft singing. But instruments vary and the beginner should experiment by trying different breath-pressures until a good-sounding note is produced. Too much breath makes a note coarse, or even causes a higher harmonic to sound: too little makes a note weak and wheezy.

The next problem is to keep the note 'straight', instead

of starting hesitantly, getting quickly loud and sharp, and then slowly and miserably trailing away to abject flatness. This requires much practice, for the breath-pressure used on the recorder is low enough to make control difficult. Keep the lungs reasonably filled and try to be conscious of the smooth and even passage of breath from the lungs, through the throat and mouth, and into the wind-channel. In the early stages do not try to play long notes, but choose to play music as fast as the fingers can comfortably manage: hymn tunes are difficult and come later. Play tunes you know, for if the tunes and, even more important, the words, are familiar, control of breath-pressure comes more easily. Above all, listen to yourself. Play into the corner of a room so that the sound is reflected back at you, or, better still, hear yourself back on a tape-recording machine.

This note you are now playing, the note E, should be short but good. Aim at a slow crotchet's length (i.e. the time between two normal heart-beats). When you are convinced the note is good, and not until, turn back to the fingering. Hammer the second finger down, and if it resounds correctly, press down hard, and blow exactly as you did for E. You can now play D and the addition of C to this repertoire creates no new difficulties. Three notes are enough to begin playing tunes such as the following:

Suo-Gân

When you can manage this comfortably, try playing it for a change with the pairs of crotchets played under one breath, that is, slurred. If a descant player of equal proficiency and a competent pianist can also be found then the way is clear to play the opening pieces in Robert Salkeld's two excellent books of *Concert Pieces* (Schott). Other pieces to play are the first parts of 'Here's a Health unto His Majesty' and 'Au Clair de la Lune', both beginning on C. Practising the recorder by playing pieces such as these is quite the pleasantest way of becoming familiar with the fingerings.

The third line of 'Au Clair de la Lune' goes outside the three notes learnt so far. It needs A, B, and G to complete it. A is two fingers below C—the first two fingers of the right hand. Locate the holes by the groping method and when the fingers have measured their position, press, pat, and hammer. Now play the note A, a good, short, straight note. Look at the fingering chart at the back of this book for the B fingering; the hammering note is this time rather indefinite but it is there. A good hammer with the third finger of the right hand with all the other fingers down for the note A will produce a very satisfactory G so long as the finger squarely covers both half-holes. Now attempt 'Au Clair de la Lune' right through. If some of the lower notes don't come, it is because one finger has slid slightly off its hole (or you are blowing too hard). Don't try and find the culprit but go right back to E and run the finger-tip lightly right round each hole (a shortened form of 'groping') and press down hard. If you are holding tightly enough this sliding off the hole should not happen. The jump from D to A in 'Au Clair de la Lune' is a little difficult, but it can be made easier by practising hammering all three fingers (third left and first and second right)—a good test of synchronization of the muscles. In the lower notes it is essential that light tonguing (a very soft 'dh') be used, and in the early stages the player will find it easier to tongue lightly if he uses a lower breath-pressure, although this must not lead him to the harmful fallacy that low notes must always be played with low breath-pressures and high notes with high. It is one of the qualities of the recorder that all the notes except the very highest will play with high and low breath-pressures (i.e. loud and soft in terms of volume). The secret is in the tonguing.

Finger G and examine the position of the right hand. As it is farther from the body the wrist is slightly angled—in other words in the side view the line down the middle finger through the wrist to the elbow is slightly bent at the wrist. The player's view of his forearm and hand should be exactly the same as for the left hand, the line from finger-tip under the arch formed by the fingers, through the centre of the wrist, and up the forearm being straight.

The turn of the wrist makes the finger that is exactly at right-angles to the instrument the third, not the second, although all three fingers are practically parallel. The right thumb, leaning against its rest, is much farther across the instrument than the left thumb, and this has the effect of pushing up the middle finger so that its main joint is slightly above finger-nail level. Nevertheless, the general impression looking down the fingers is that of a plateau formed by the backs of the fingers. The attitude of the hands and fingers should be as comfortable and natural as possible, with only such twists and bends as are unavoidable, for when the hands and fingers are straight and parallel the muscles are more relaxed and equality of finger movement is easier to achieve. The finger that is in the least natural position is the first of the right hand, on which the mark of the hole appears considerably offset to the right of centre: some recorder-makers have minimized this one awkwardness of recorder fingering by cutting the hole on the oblique, although this has a slightly adverse effect on tone-quality.

With these three new notes come wider vistas. The player can now pick out such tunes as 'Jingle Bells' (starting on B), 'Baa, Baa, Black Sheep' (G), and, for a change, the middle section of the 'Skye Boat Song' (E), with its difficult D to A slur.

The player should resist the temptation to play the bottom note of the recorder, which can be a very frustrating business, and turn his attention again to the left hand. Up to now, the first finger and thumb have been held firmly down, but a glance at the fingering chart will show that for F^1 the first finger must be lifted. Practise the transition from E to F^1, a sort of walking movement. At this stage do not attempt to slur these two notes but keep them well separated. When a good F^1 has been made, just for once try the effect of slurring from E to F^1, and from F^1 to E. You will find that it is hard to avoid making a clicking sound by the intercalation of a short 'in-between note' (either D or $F\sharp^1$). One of the chief problems of recorder technique is to learn how to avoid 'clicks', as they are ugly and can ruin phrasing.

To go from F^1 to G^1, all that has to be done is to take the thumb from its hole. It is at this stage that the importance of the thumb-rest is appreciated, as the firmness of the second finger of the left hand pressing on its hole should be maintained. Having played a good G^I try F$\sharp^I$. Watch breath-pressure used for these strong-sounding notes at the centre of the recorder's compass, for blowing too hard makes them coarse in tone, G^I particularly so.

The player now has at his command a whole G major scale plus an extra note (F$\natural^I$), and this achievement should be celebrated by a prolonged bout of tune playing. Try 'The First Nowell' (starting on B), 'Now is the Month of Maying' (C), 'Robin Adair' (G), 'For He's a Jolly Good Fellow' (G), 'Clementine' (C), 'Barbara Allen' (G), Brahms's 'Cradle Song' (B), and 'Bobby Shaftoe' (C). Better still, find other players of equal proficiency with whom you can play rounds such as 'London's Burning' (starting on G), James Hook's delightful *Easy Lessons for descant and treble recorders*, Nos. 1–7 (Schott), or trios such as those in Bergmann's *School Ensemble Book*. The best solo practice possible is country dance tunes as they compel accuracy of rhythm and demand finger dexterity. A start can be made on 'The Coronation Day', 'The Happy Clown', and 'Scotland' in *Tunes from 'The Dancing Master'* (arr. Monica Dewey—Schott). Nearly all of Salkeld's *Concert Pieces* are now within the player's capacity.

In making the note B, the principle of 'cross-fingering' is used. B is a semitone flatter than C, and the flattening of C is effected by leaving the hole immediately below it open but covering the next two. Exactly the same method is used to obtain E$\flat$ and D$\flat$ (or C$\sharp$). The principle is also applied in the fingering for B$\flat$. A beginner who started the recorder by going down the scale of F major would expect the fingering for B$\flat$ to be the thumb and three fingers of the left hand and the first of the right (or, in fingering shorthand, 0 123 4–––), and this is indeed the case with some pre-war German instruments which tried to simplify B$\flat$ but which only succeeded in making B$\natural$ a difficult note to finger (see p. 91). With so-called 'baroque' or 'English' fingering the note produced with 0 123 4––– is too sharp for B$\flat$ (and rather flat for B$\natural$—see p. 79), and it has therefore to be flattened by missing a hole and adding two fingers below so that its fingering becomes 0 123 4–67. These cross-fingered notes need the lightest of tonguings.

The B♮ fingering brings the little finger into action and once again the 'grope, press, pat, and hammer' method is essential. Before starting to find bottom F make sure you have a perfect G. Hold the fingers firmly and strike the little finger down really hard when you reach the hammering stage. The percussive note formed is quite impressive. It is important that both half-holes are completely covered, and careful adjustment should be made of the exact position of the foot-joint of the instrument until the holes are in the most comfortable place. Remember that the flat pad of the finger must be used, so it is necessary for the little finger, unlike any of the others, to be straight from the knuckle. Tonguing for bottom F should be light, but once the note has begun quite high breath-pressure can be used on it. When the transition from G to F has been mastered, practise the interval A to F, and then C to F moving all the fingers of the left hand together. A good exercise for getting bottom F (but an exasperating one at first attempt), is to alternate F with the notes of its scale, thus:

The factor that makes the recorder superior to other fipple-flutes is the use of the thumb-hole as an 'octaving' hole. The principle is that the opening of a small hole in the upper part of the instrument causes the sound waves within the instrument to halve in length and so produce a note an octave higher. This small hole is made by putting the thumb-nail into the thumb-hole and pressing it against the side of the hole, leaving the remainder of the hole covered with the fleshy tip of the thumb, so that only a chink of space remains open between the thumb-nail and the edge of the hole. This chink should be about a tenth of the total area of the thumb-hole. The movement from the covered position to the 'thumbed' position should be a

very slight one if the thumb is correctly placed when covering its hold: the move is effected by bending the thumb-
joint so that the thumb-nail is nearly vertical to the hole.
A beginner on the recorder should deliberately pinch his
thumb-nail against the side of the hole (in most tutors the
process is called 'pinching'), but as skill in thumbing is
acquired the thumb should become more relaxed so that
the thumb-nail feels it is only resting against the side of the
thumb-hole.   The first thumbed note that should be
attempted is C^I (three fingers of the left hand). It should
be given a strong tonguing—'doo' instead of 'dhoo', and
a slightly higher breath-pressure than notes in the lower
octave. Try next the note D^I. Its beginning will not be so
clear as C^I, but do not worry at the moment for it can be
perfected at a later stage. Now, making sure that all the
fingers are firmly covering their holes, play A^I. It will be
found that this note also plays without the use of the thumb
at all, but the tone-quality is better with thumbing and that
is the normal fingering.

Cross-fingering to flatten a note is more critical in the
upper octave, and it is therefore only necessary to put one
finger on below the hole left open to lower a note by a
semitone. B♮^{I} is therefore fingered ∅ 123 –5––, C♯^{I}
∅ 12– 4–––, and B♭^{I} ∅ 123 4–6–. Two of these notes
require care in playing: B♭^{I} can have an obstreperous
tone-quality and must, like G^I, not be given too much
breath-pressure, and C♯^{I} dislikes strong tonguing so must
be given a lighter tonguing than C^I or D^I. Heavy cross-
fingerings slightly overblown produce the highest notes of
the recorder which should be learnt in the order E♭^{I}, E^I,
F^{II}, and G^{II} (see fingering chart). Beginners will hardly
ever be required to use them and their mastery should be
left for a later stage.

The remaining three notes needed to complete two
chromatic octaves should now be learnt. A♭^{I} (– –23 456–)
is a loud note like G and should be treated with circum-
spection. Bottom A♭ and F♯ are obtained by using the
half-holes on 6 and 7. Do not try to cover these half-holes
by bending the finger up, but instead move the whole
right hand round so that the half-holing finger is in exactly

the same relative position as it is when covering all the hole. The pivoting of the hand brings the first finger (4) so far round that it is lying alongside and touching the instrument right up to its main joint. In this position carry out the usual 'grope, press, pat, and hammer' exercise for A♭. Moving the hand back to a point half-way between the A♭ position and normal, practise F♯ in the same way. Now play F—F♯—G—A♭—A—B♭ and watch first the level of the fingers—the effect of plateau should never be broken, and then the gradual turning of the back of the hand and its resumption of normal position on B♭.

Fingering in the early stages should always be deliberate, almost violent. The unused fingers should be lifted high and the player should be aware of the clatter of his fingers as they strike the instrument. Every movement must be quick and neat. Greater delicacy of fingering will come with experience. Difficult finger moves, e.g. D—E♭—F, will be met with in tune-playing. The player should then stop and practise the difficult series of notes over and over again until the finger movement is neat and quick enough for the offending notes to be played as a slur, without 'clicks'. When a slur is marked in the music (as, for example, over the first two notes of 'The First Nowell'), *always* play the slur under one breath with no tonguing on the second note. With difficult slurs a recorder player is tempted to break the slur with tonguing, but to do so is cheating. Slurring and legato playing provide the best means of learning dexterity of fingering—the fingers have to move more quickly to slur two minims in an Adagio than to play two unslurred semiquavers in an Allegro.

With two chromatic scales at his command the player is fully fledged, and the wide world of recorder music is before him. As recorder playing is a social activity (or should be) he should now find other players of recorders and other instruments, and join or form a consort. His technique is already, after so little hard work, enough to enable him to give a competent account of a middle line in most consort music—in fact it is probably far in advance of his capabilities as a musician. He should let himself be carried away on this first wave of the excitement of being able to join in making great music, of giving utterance to the written notes of Palestrina, Morley, Byrd, and Dowland, and then he will rapidly gain experience of music itself, and learn how it is formed and phrased. In this delectable process of habituation and discovery the recorder player should make his guiding rule: 'Be confident, but never be complacent'.

V

BREATHING

Two factors affect how one breathes in order to play a wind-instrument—first the expenditure of breath needed to make a note, and secondly the pressure required. In oboe playing breathing is a major problem as the instrument uses a small amount of air at a high pressure, and this is true to varying degrees with most other wind instruments. Recorders, however, 'go with a gentle breath', using as much air and at as low a pressure as is needed for reading aloud or soft singing. Were it not for the fact that intake of air must be very much more rapid than exhalation, it could be said that in playing the recorder one breathes naturally. Recorder playing is just unnatural enough to cause breathlessness or indigestion if it is indulged in immediately after eating or drinking.

Breathing for recorder playing, as for singing and playing other wind-instruments, should be from the bottom of the lungs, that is, the diaphragm. Sit or stand upright with the shoulders back and the head up, and become conscious of the movement of the muscle across the triangle formed by the ribs below the breast-bone. Breathe in deeply through the nose so that the diaphragm is fully extended but do not raise or hunch the shoulders in the process: then, with your hand on the diaphragm, release the air in five or six separate and fairly slow exhalations, noting the muscular movement. Now open the mouth and, moving the diaphragm only, draw in a good breath as quickly as possible so that the lungs are nearly full. Half close the lips and let the air go out softly, slowly, and evenly. Notice that in breathing in both directions the muscles of the throat and mouth do nothing: they remain relaxed so that air can be pumped past them by the diaphragm. It is easy to fall into the bad habit of snatching a small amount of breath in quickly with the throat—that is, gasping—when a breath has to be taken during a very short interval in the music: it is vital, however, that even when time allows only a little replenishment of the lungs the action should come from the diaphragm.

The impression one should have when blowing into the recorder is that the breath originates from the base of the lungs, a sensation of air forced up from underneath and travelling smoothly up the wind-pipe, through the throat, across the mouth and without hindrance into the windway of the recorder. The conscious realization of this sensation of the passage of the air from the diaphragm to the edge helps to keep a long note steady. If you have difficulty in experiencing the sensation, artificially create conditions in which the diaphragm has to pump harder by making a stricture in your mouth with your tongue against your teeth, and feel the push of the air up to the stricture, which reduces pressure, and through to the instrument. As an aid towards playing a long note evenly this device would be more useful if it did not disturb the air-flow and create unwanted eddies that affect tone (see pp. 44 and 107); it can serve a purpose, however, where very quiet long notes are required as diaphragm control at ultra-low pressures is extremely difficult and in such circumstances good tone must be sacrificed for steady intonation. Some further assistance in keeping a long note steady can be gained by imagining that the note is being sung, quietly, to the sound 'oo'. Once a note is started the tongue should always return to this 'oo' position, in which the tongue and the lips are best placed for good tone-production.

When playing a piece of music, a recorder player should feel all the time that his lungs are reasonably full, though never bursting. No opportunity where a breath might be taken should be allowed to go by unused. All rests are breath-marks. Aim at breathing frequently even if only a little at a time, so that occasions where a big (and noisy) inhalation takes place are rare. It is particularly important to breathe often and deeply when playing bass instruments: breathlessness causes anxiety both to performers and audience. With a sopranino the condition might arise where a lungful of air becomes stale before it is used up, and like an oboist, the player has to breathe both out and in at the end of a long phrase.

Breath-pressure

Generally speaking, recorder players tend to blow too hard—high breath-pressures are only needed for solos, and then not invariably. Practise like this: finger the note G^1 on the treble, and, after breathing in deep, whisper into the instrument to make the quietest noise you can manage that passes for a musical note. Hold it *steady* (this is very difficult) for twenty seconds; don't let it get out of control at the end. Now play the same note loud like a trumpet, giving it the greatest breath-pressure you dare, almost making the note 'break'—that is overblow with a nasty rasp into a higher octave. Hold the note steady for ten seconds (this is relatively easy) and finish by blowing it over the break. The first note will be thin and wispy, the second strident, and the two should be at least a whole tone apart in pitch, more on a good wooden recorder. Now go back to the low breath-pressure but make the note just loud enough to be pleasant and convincing (it will still, however, be a little breathy): this is your instrument's '*pp*'. A clean, loud (but still slightly harsh) note well clear of that break you have just discovered, is your '*ff*'. Somewhere between the two pressures, generally but not necessarily midway, lies the most beautiful G^1—find it by experiment —and this is your optimum breath-pressure. In consort playing, however, your general level of attack should be slightly below this pressure, so that your purest notes come in an '*mf*' passage or when you announce a theme in a Fancy.

When you have found your best G^1, move on to other notes on the instrument, studying their behaviour under varying breath-pressures. You will thereby discover the level of pressure at which your recorder plays best. Different recorders are voiced to play best at different breath-pressures so be prepared to vary the general level of attack to suit each instrument.

To consolidate these experiments play at low, high, and medium pressures and at a speed of about five seconds to each note any slow hymn-tune made up of equal length notes (e.g. 'Rock of Ages' starting on C). Practise on all the recorders you have and concentrate on steady breathing at low pressures—it is more salutary to your own playing and kinder to the neighbours. Practise into a mirror, or, if you are shy, towards the corner of a room, so that the sound is reflected back at you; concentrate very hard on listening to it (would that more musicians did this!) and be extremely critical. Do not allow a waver in the evenness of your sound.

Having established the optimum breath-pressure for each note practise the rapid change in breath-pressure required when slurring from a note in the lower octave to a note in the upper octave above the 'break' in registers, e.g. F¹ to A¹. To avoid 'clicks' (see p. 47) two conditions are essential—extreme rapidity of finger movement and a sudden though small increase in breath-pressure from the optimum for F¹ to the optimum for A¹. Some recorders behave better than others with awkward slurs over the register break: a player who can do these slurs on any instrument pianissimo without 'clicks' may claim to be an expert.

Another breath-pressure technique that must be mastered is the tiny decrescendo that finishes the last note of a phrase: it must be so miniature that a listener does not get the impression of the note going flat. A momentary holding-back of breath-pressure is also useful in negotiating difficult slurs, for, if breath-pressure is reduced for that fraction of a second when the fingers are moving, 'clicks' are made less prominent if they do occur. Practise wide slurs such as F¹ to B♭ or D¹ to F¹ and notice how 'in-between notes' can be eliminated by breath-pressure control.

Vibrato

Recorder players who, anxious to obtain the best and most characteristic tone-quality their instrument will produce, sensibly seek to improve their breath-control by reading books on vocal technique, will discover that Norris Croker, in his excellent *Handbook for Singers* (Augener), lists vibrato as a defect caused by nervous debility. This harsh judgement probably stems from the fact that vibrato can develop into a bad habit if it is used without modulation and discretion. To a recorder player, vibrato is as

important as it is to a string player. Its use is discussed in
Chapter XI (p. 108): its production is described here.

Vibrato is produced by alternately decreasing and
increasing breath-pressure, regularly and rapidly. Although
vibrato can be effected by tongue or finger movements (the
'close shake' as advocated by Hotteterre), the best way of
producing it is from the back of the throat, or, when a
throbbing cantabile effect is desired, from the source of the
air-flow, that is to say, the diaphragm. The action may
be represented by the syllables 'hu-hu-hu-hu-hu-hu'
aspirated deep in the throat without any interruption in the
actual flow of air. The effect is easiest obtained on a
sopranino or descant at high breath-pressure. Start with a
'long wave-length' (slow 'hu-hu's') and increase the
frequency until you get a 'short wave-length' of vibrations
—this is the natural vibrato that some beginners produce
without realizing it (they find it all the harder to play a
plain note without vibrato). Once the knack is acquired
(and it is deceptively easy) you will soon settle down to a
comfortable short wave-length vibrato, and you should be
producing much more convincing notes than you did
without vibrato. Never let vibrato become entirely auto-
matic. Continue to practise long notes without it (they are
much harder to control without vibrato just as it is more
difficult to balance on a bicycle without slight wobbling):
playing without vibrato or with very little indeed is essential
in medieval music and in most consort playing. Practise
also the other extreme, slow vibrato (long wave-length):
aim at keeping the vibrations steady and even at about
six to a second without getting any quicker, continuing to
use a high breath-pressure to aid control. Attempt, too,
something between this slow vibrato and your normal
rapid vibrato (call this 'medium wave-length'). The
following diagram may clarify matters; note that the 'long
wave-length' vibrato is wider in its fluctuations than the
'short wave-length' vibrato:

long wave-length:

medium wave-length:

short wave-length:
no vibrato:

Try the effect of beginning a note without vibrato, then introducing into its thin texture a small and very rapid vibrato which gradually slows down and widens into a full-bodied long-wave vibrato; this exercise is easier if the note swells in volume at the same time. Apply the three vibrato wave-lengths to your hymn-tune practice, playing at the three different breath-pressures. Counting the plain note, this gives twelve ways of playing the same hymn-tune: listening very minutely to what you are doing, try them all. If you work hard, for the process of mastering all twelve interpretations is a gruelling one, you will find that the simple recorder becomes in your hands a truly expressive instrument.

VI

TONGUING

The last chapter described only the process of making the middle part of a note. This deals with the beginning and ending of a note on a recorder—how to 'give it breath with your mouth', and to take it away.

Most recorder players, in their enthusiasm to get on with the job, tongue too hard. Perhaps, however, they have been misled at the very beginning by those tutors that tell players to pronounce 't' into the instrument to start a note. This instruction, possibly inherited from flute tutors, has two bad effects, firstly that it explodes too much air into the instrument at once, thus starting a note too sharp, or even starting the wrong note (by overblowing), and secondly that, with Gallic precision, it deposits nodules of spit neatly across the edge so ruining tone, or causing a complete blockage. Apart from these purely hydrostatic phenomena, you can always tell the 't' addicts because when they play G¹ they start somewhere near A♭¹ and then either lurch down to G¹ or persist in playing A♭¹ very loud. If they aim at C♯¹ they get E¹, and many of their notes, particularly bottom ones, have to clear their throats before they speak.

The consonant to aim at for normal tonguing is 'dh' (see p. 44), obtained by placing the tongue in the position to say 'd' but then at the last moment changing it to 'h'. It is a very soft sound, almost imperceptibly a consonant. Yet, within limits, it can vary in strength (compare the 'dh' sounds made in 'dhar', 'dher', and 'dhee').

Strong tonguing is easy to do—in fact those very words 'to do' are instances of it, 'd' being strong tonguing on the recorder with 't' used only as very strong tonguing. Both 'd' and 't', like 'dh', may be played with different degrees of 'explosion', so extending the useful range of tonguings. Light tonguing, softer than 'dh', is harder to master, but its acquisition is imperative for playing the lowest notes of the recorder and any notes requiring cross-fingerings ('forked' or 'gapped' fingerings), e.g. low B♭, E♭, high E$^{|}$, etc. The more fingers that are below the hole left open the lighter the tonguing required. Try for example, the notes produced by the fingering 0 –23 4567; with the faintest tonguing imaginable the note should be somewhat near B♭, while a slightly more definite tonguing should give F♯$^{|}$. Observe that the note produced seems to depend more on the tonguing than on the breath-pressure used. Now, taking off a half-hole at a time and using the very faint tonguing, play a series of notes that will be in the vicinity of B♮, C, C♯, and D. Once struck, play them as loudly as you can without causing them to break upwards. In the slightly stronger tonguing you should get a similar range of less than semitones from F♯$^{|}$ to A$^{|}$: once struck, play them softly. This illustrates the important principle that strength of tonguing does not necessarily vary with breath-pressure. Practise jumping from one 'register' to the other in quick succession over the five pairs of notes: do this so that each note speaks clearly and immediately.

To appreciate gradations of tonguing from light to strong try the following exercise. Starting with a good lungful of air play, without vibrato, the note G$^{|}$, keeping the tongue still. Gradually move the tongue backward and forward without quite letting it touch the teeth-ridge: this introduces 'tongue vibrato' into the note (see p. 64). Now bring the tongue movements forward so that the tip of the tongue touches the ridge, impeding but not quite stopping the flow of breath: this is the 'r' position of tonguing, the lightest possible. Bring the tongue further forward, coming to the 'l' position in which air escapes only round the side of the tongue. Next close up to the soft 'dh' position (normal tonguing) and finally strengthen the tonguing to the most violent 'd' and 't' positions. Practise the exercise in reverse, and on different notes. Volume should remain constant (either soft, loud, or between) during the exercise. If 'oo' is used to show the flow of breath after tonguing, the exercise may be expressed thus: 'too-doo-dhoo-loo-roo-yoo-oo', each syllable being repeated three or four times. Early writers of recorder tutors (e.g. Ganassi and Hotteterre) use 't', 'd', 'l', and 'r' to describe tonguing strengths in various musical contexts: an excellent summary of these writers' methods is contained in Hildemarie Peter's *The Recorder—its traditions and its tasks* (translated by Stanley Godman in 1958 and published by Lienau—Hinrichsen D 1192) a book which should be read for a fuller and more historical account of recorder playing than it is appropriate to give here.

Certain notes on the recorder require very careful tonguing. One of these is $C\sharp^{l}$, or, even more pertinently, $G\sharp^{l}$ on the tenor. This is a peculiarly slow-speaking note and unless it is tongued very gently will either cough before speaking or will strike a tone and a half too high. Passages where this note has to be repeated rapidly need cautious treatment, and it is wise not to break the flow of air after the first tonguing, saying, as it were, 'dhoo-yoo-yoo-yoo' instead of 'dhoo-dhoo-dhoo-dhoo'. The same is true of repeated high F^{ll}s. Special tonguings are needed for the highest notes of the recorder, including 'whoot' for the very high C^{ll} (see Chapter IX). A trick to soften tonguing, particularly when breath-pressures are high (e.g. in a series of high notes) is to breathe out momentarily through the nose at the same time as tonguing. This is a useful anti-panic device when a high F^{ll} is looming up.

Attack: portamento and staccato

The two extremes in tonguing are a long note with strong tonguing, and a short note with a light tonguing. Between them lies a wide vocabulary of different ways of treating a note, each suited to a particular context. Tonguing, which is analogous to 'attack', combines with variation in the length and volume of notes to create rhythm. In a bar of four crotchets in common time all on the same note, rhythm is established by the degree of attack accorded to each note. The attack on the first note is more definite, and it is played longer and louder than any of the remaining three: a secondary emphasis is placed on the third note, while the last is the slackest, shortest, and quietest of the four. On the note G^{l} practise bars containing one note-value in 4/4 time, 3/4, 6/8, and slow 2/4 ('One—and—two—and'), and by using variations in tonguing, length of note and volume, establish rhythms. Try this at different speeds, and different styles between legato and staccato, from *ff* to *pp*. Then attempt to do the same thing with tonguing only, using notes of equal length and loudness. If, *using tonguing only* and playing only the note G¹, you can communicate to a friend the differences between a 4/4 bar and a 2/4 bar at the same speed in quavers, or between a 6/8 bar and two 3/4 bars at the same speed, you have acquired the ultimate subtlety in tonguing control. Gradation of attack such as that which differentiates

from

by means only of tonguing illustrates nuances of technique in the service of interpretation.

Long notes barely separated by light tonguing constitute 'portamento', the word deriving from the fact that one note is all but carried over, or slurred, to the next. The musical indication is

although portamento tonguing is used for playing any legato passage: in one with a series of notes of equal written length, such as the example quoted, the effect should be such that the 'dhoo' tonguing almost becomes 'lhoo'. The tongue itself should be made to feel soft and flabby in portamento tonguing, only just grazing the roof of the mouth for each note. Fingering must be quick or the notes will trip over each other. Portamento is an important technique to acquire not only for its interpretative applications but also because the ability to tongue with an infinitesimal interruption of sound is invaluable in suggesting a slur over notes that would (for lack of alternative fingering) be extremely difficult to slur properly without 'clicks'. An instance where this form of deceit might be used is the following bar from No. 8 of 'Fifteen Solos' (Schott Ed. 2562A):

Only the most brilliant players could play this slur perfectly without any suggestion of sound other than its three notes. With a touch of tonguing between the notes the player can eliminate 'clicks' and deceive most listeners into hearing a slur, particularly if he plays the remaining three notes of the phrase fairly staccato.

Staccato may be considered the converse of portamento since it consists of short notes played with strong to medium tonguing. One of its developments is 'echo tonguing'. This is the recorder's equivalent to the harp pedal on the harpsichord and is used for echo effects in passage work. Echo tonguing is produced by pressing the tongue firmly on the teeth-ridge (in the 'd' position) and releasing it momentarily and only enough to allow a little air to pass to produce a short and stifled note. The impression to the player is that his tongue is almost drowning the sound of the instrument by the noise of its activity.

Double and compound tonguings

Double tonguing is achieved by alternating the 'dh' sounds with 'gh', giving an effect 'dhoo-ghoo-dhoo-ghoo' or at speed 'dugger-dugger-dugger-dugger'. When first acquiring the knack do it slowly and deliberately, giving plenty of breath to the 'gh' sound: it will sound ugly at first, but will become more convincing as speed increases. Practise on one note first, then two adjacent notes beginning on the upper; then transfer your attentions to scales and to passage work. Finally, learn to do it smoothly and regularly and be able to apply it to fast legato passages in the form of double-tongued portamento (dhoo-roo-lhoo-roo).

The chief value of double tonguing is to avoid getting tongue-tied in passage work. The more expert a player becomes the greater control he gains over single tonguing and he may discard double tonguing in passages of moderate speed where previously he found it a boon. In very fast passages, however, it must always be used, e.g. in Telemann's Trio-Sonatas in G minor and D minor (Schott). Double tonguing has the excellent secondary effect of evening-up wayward rhythms, due to the pairing of the notes and the placing of an accent on the 'dh' note. It is invaluable in playing four isolated semiquavers nicely in time as well as pairs of semiquavers which might otherwise get rushed. Double tonguing can smooth out a three-semiquaver entry to a phrase, which should be pronounced 'ghoo-dhoo-ghoo' with an accent on the 'dhoo': the pattern is often met with in overtures in the French style. In most contexts in eighteenth-century music the time-value of a dotted note is longer than it is in modern music; conversely, the short note following a dotted note is played shorter than it is written (a useful rule of thumb is that the short note takes up one-ninth of the beat in which it occurs). With the tonguing 'd-dhoo' this very short note tends to be muffled, but the double tonguing 'g-dhoo' gives a clearer and tauter enunciation, and encourages a forward impetus in dotted rhythms.

Triple tonguing is pronounced 'dh-gh-dh, gh-dh-gh', or, in the form of a mnemonic, 'do good to gaudy girl'; with lighter tonguing triple tonguing is enunciated 'diddly-diddly'. Another method is 'dh-gh-dh, dh-gh-dh'. It is seldom needed in the recorder's repertoire, although it must be used in Vivaldi's 'Tempesta di Mare' Concerto (S. Ant) in which there are triplets of great velocity. The last movement of the same concerto contains bars where the speed is too great for any 'dh-gh' formula, and the player has to fall back on something like 'diddle-iddle-iddle' or to use a slur with tongue vibrato.

Tongue vibrato is a kind of divided slur that may be represented 'dhoo-yoo-yoo-yoo-yoo . . .'. It separates the notes of a slur without actually breaking the flow of air but produces the semblance of unslurred notes. It is in effect the same technique as the special $C\sharp^1$ tonguing mentioned earlier, except that it is applied to very fast runs or slurs which threaten to become a mess under normal treatment. An example is the express-train chromatic run in Lennox Berkeley's Sonatina (S): the second half of the same bar of pyrotechnics calls for a scurry of double tonguing.

Flutter tonguing is possible on the recorder. It consists of trilling the tongue against the roof of the mouth in the manner of an extended rolled 'r': a fairly high breath-pressure is needed. To date, it is used only in Stanley Taylor's arrangement of Clive Richardson's 'Beachcomber' (Boosey and Hawkes), and in Benjamin Britten's *Noyes Fludde* to imitate the cooing of the dove.

Ending a note

Ordinarily, there are no difficulties. The return of the tongue into the correct 'dh' position effortlessly and efficiently both stops one note and prepares for the next.

Difficulties arise when there is no next note. They mount still more if the last note of a phrase, or worse still of a whole piece, happens to be a long note. If this last long note is marked *ff* the odds are that the player will swoop up an exuberant semitone in a final burst of defiance to the composer, and if it is marked *pp* he will expire a semitone flat with appalling pathos. Control must be retained till the very end of a piece of music—and a second or two more. If the last note makes demands on the lungs a little vibrato will help to keep it steady. The actual stopping of the note may be done in the normal way of putting the tongue back to the 'dh' position with great speed and delicacy; if the note is very quiet and therefore hard to control, the tongue may come forward into the 'lh' position while it is being played, the stop then being made by a quick forward and upward pressure of the tongue.

Another way is to cut off the air with the lips, plucking the recorder from the mouth at the same time. The lips should close firmly and instantaneously behind the instrument. This method is surprisingly effective, both aurally and visually.

VII

INTONATION

A note is in tune when it bears a perfect relation to the notes preceding and following it (melody) and to other notes being played at the same time (harmony). A person can only achieve an understanding of the relationship of one note to another by listening to music in such a way that he hears all the separate strands of a piece of music (preferably by concentrating on the middle voice and remaining aware of the treble and bass) and is at the same time conscious of the construction of each chord. A recorder player can only keep in tune, therefore, if as well as playing his own part he listens to everyone else's. If his part is too hard or the structure of the music too complex for him to do this, he should at least listen to one other part, and that should be either the bass or the part next below. Intonation is always improved in a consort if the players sit in the order of their parts. Only by listening carefully along and through a piece of music as a whole can such justness of intonation be achieved as the narrowing of the semitone between a leading-note and its tonic, or the flattening of minor and sharpening of major thirds and sixths. It is important that a note or a chord should be imagined in the mind's ear before it is played; no true musician will embark upon playing a note without knowing what it is. This chapter, therefore, describes the means at a recorder player's disposal of communicating the exact note he has in mind.

Whatever beginners might learn, the thumb and first three fingers of the left hand on the treble recorder do not necessarily produce a definite note C. If the instrument is 'in tune' and warm, and if the player uses medium breath-pressure, he will, however, produce one of the many notes that are conveniently represented by a mark on the second space down on the treble stave, rather than one that would be better represented by the same mark with a sharp or a flat in front of it. The player has the power to cover the whole range of notes that are expressed by this C, starting from the territory uneasily shared with B right up to the foothills of C♯. He has the freedom of the singer or the violinist, and is not confined, like the pianist, to pressing a key and taking what comes.

The experiments in breath-pressure advocated in Chapter V (p. 55) will have shown that on the note G^I the range of intonation is, on most recorders, a whole tone or slightly more. The intonation range of notes above or below G^I is rather less, but even on top F^{II} or bottom F most recorders will range well over a semitone. The fact that recorder intonation is so sensitive to changes in breath-pressure is both an advantage and a disadvantage. It is an advantage in so far as small alterations in breath-pressure will move the pitch of a note slightly without a significant effect on the volume of sound produced. This enables the player to make minor corrections to the pitch of a note either to keep in tune with other players or to overcome imperfections natural to his own instrument. A treble player might, for example, find that his F^I was a little flat and would correct it by blowing harder. One comes to make these modifications automatically when the idio-syncrasies of a particular recorder are known—indeed they must be made on every recorder for it is neither possible nor desirable that a recorder should be constructed absolutely in tune throughout its chromatic register with a stable breath-pressure.

This admirable flexibility of intonation reaches its limits when the changes in breath-pressure become great enough to affect volume: it is obviously musically undesirable that a player with a very flat F^I should blurt it out loud (but in tune) every time he comes to it. Conversely, the sensitivity of intonation to breath-pressure becomes a disadvantage when variations in volume are called for by the composer or by the style of the music. True echo effects, for example, are delightful, but not if the 'echo' is a semitone flat.

Shading and shade-fingering

The chief technique for flattening a note is called 'shading'. To shade a note means to lower the unused

fingers over the open holes until the note is flattened to the
extent desired. As an experiment play the note E on the
treble loudly and lower the second finger of the left hand
over its hole until the stream of air coming from the hole
can be felt on the ball of the finger. Now, lowering the
finger slowly, press this column of air down into the hole
until the finger is just grazing the edges of the hole. Very
gradually press the finger home to complete your slide
down from E to D. Shading with the uppermost unused
finger is extremely critical as a tiny movement affects the
note's pitch, and it is less nerve-racking to impinge upon
the lesser columns of air emerging from holes lower down:
the whole process of shading E with the third finger of the
left hand cannot lower it as much as a semitone, and the
first finger of the right hand has less than a quartertone
effect. It is perhaps best to shade with all the fingers at one's
disposal. Try playing E and moving the unused fingers up
and down to produce a controlled, slow, wavering effect
reminiscent of American railway engine whistles. In this
exercise the fingers of the right hand may actually cover
their holes, but the two left-hand shading fingers have to
be moved with more care and should never be low enough
to touch the instrument. Another method of shading is to
place the shading finger on the instrument but at the side
of its hole, from where it may roll over towards the hole as
required. This method is particularly useful when only one
finger is available to do the shading; an example is bottom
G which is sometimes a little sharp and can be flattened by
placing the little finger, politely bent, on the brink of its
half-hole. Middle G$^|$ is another note that is often sharp, and
although it can be shaded from above the easiest way to
flatten it is to lean the first finger of the left hand against
the side of the instrument, keeping the finger quite straight
and jutting out over the hole in such a position that bending
the top joint causes extra flattening. The other fingers lie
low, and the little finger may actually be on its hole, partly
to keep the instrument steady.

Shading may be achieved by covering holes left open,
provided that the hole taking the shade-fingering is low
down on the instrument in relation to the position of the

fingers making the note itself. The most useful fingers for this method of shading are the little finger and the third finger of the right hand, for the degrees of flattening they control are made finer by their double-holes. Little-finger shading is the most delicate of all: shading a note such as E or F^1 with the little finger scarcely lowers the pitch, but the little finger comes into its own not only on lower notes such as A or C but in the upper octave where the effects of shading are accentuated (compare the effect of adding the little finger to the ordinary B♭^{1} fingering with the same movement an octave down). Another form of shading is the covering of a hole below an ordinary 'forked' fingering. Many recorders, for example, produce a sharp C♯ with the usual fingering (0 12– 45––), and the third finger of the right hand has to cover its hole or half-hole to bring the note into tune. Alternatively, if the sharpness is slight, little-finger shading may be applied. Another method is to lower the third finger of the left hand into the air-stream emerging from the open hole beneath it to produce the same flattening effect; control may be gained by resting the little finger of the left hand against the side of the recorder. The choice of method depends on which comes easiest to the player, though it is generally advisable for shade-fingerings to be applied to notes that are consistently out of tune while the other methods of shading are used for temporary corrections resulting from the exigencies of consort playing, the use of remote keys or the need to play a passage loudly without sharpening.

Slide-fingering

Sharpening a note without increasing breath-pressure may be achieved by 'slide-fingering'. This simply means pulling the lowest of the fingers forming a note to one side to expose some or all of the hole it covered. It is easy enough to do this on a note that is normally a forked fingering, such as B♭ or E♭: it is simple, too, in the 'pinched' notes of the upper register, for if the thumb-hole aperture is widened the note is slightly sharpened—but care must be taken not to overdo this, otherwise the nodal effect of the pinched hole is spoilt and the note breaks downwards with an ugly crack. Intense concentration is needed, however, if a plain-fingered note such as C is sharpened, for a hair's-breadth moving of the third finger from its hole will send the note up. Control is enhanced if the operating finger is pressed firmly on to the instrument so that every edge of the hole except the fraction being released is felt as the finger is dragged sideways. Alternatively, the finger may be moved upwards, that is, lifted so as to rest lightly on the hole rather than properly cover it, but this method, even more than that of slide-fingering proper, adversely affects tone-quality—the good round sound of the plain-fingered note is weakened as the pitch rises. It is a device to which one must have recourse only *in extremis*.

Refingering

Some notes may be played sharper or flatter by re-fingering them—in other words using one of the alternative fingerings that are dealt with in detail in the next chapter. To illustrate the possibilities and complexities of intonation control let us consider the note F^1. Its normal fingering (i.e. thumb and second finger of the left hand) is often a trifle flat. It is easy to make it flatter either by shading with the first or third fingers (or both) of the left hand or by using any of the twelve feasible shade-fingerings available in the right hand. It is not, however, an easy note to sharpen, for slide-fingerings in this position are almost impossibly critical. But there are plenty of alternative fingerings for F^1, with and without the thumb. Here are some of them:

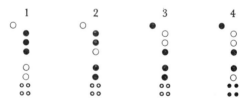

1 and 3 are the important alternatives. 1 varies considerably from one instrument to another, but generally gives either the same pitch as the normal fingering or is slightly

sharper. It can, of course, be flattened by shading either with the thumb (too critical to be safe) or the first finger of the right hand, or by shade-fingering, the most useful being with the second finger of the right hand. As it is a forked fingering it is amenable to sharpening by slide-fingering. If 1 is flat, however, the variant of it shown in 2 can be used, and this, being a double fork, is extremely easy to sharpen further by slide-fingering if necessary. 3 may be a little flat, but, because it is what one may call a 'wide fork' (there being two middle holes left open), it is less critical to slide-fingering and one, or even both, of the right hand fingers may be taken off without sending it up to F$\sharp$[1]. 4 bears the same relation to 3 as 2 does to 1 and is therefore a little sharper than 3. With experimentation you will find at least thirty fingerings (excluding half-holes) that produce some version of the note F[1]. Most of the middle notes of the recorder behave similarly. Even though low and high notes offer less opportunity for variations of fingering, intonation control of some kind is obtainable with every note on the recorder. A thoroughly bad recorder, therefore, can be played perfectly in tune, though the result would not justify mastering the difficulties.

Tuning: devices and gadgets

There is no point in knowing how to play in tune if one's instrument is basically out of tune with the other instruments in an ensemble. The first requirement of a consort is that all the recorders should be warm (see also p. 105). The motion of sound waves becomes more rapid in warm air, and the resultant rise in pitch is not compensated for by the expansion of the instrument as it gets warmer with the player's breath. A cold recorder, therefore, plays flat.

As it is easier to flatten a note than to sharpen it, the obvious rule for playing with other recorders is to tune to one's flattest note (at medium breath-pressure). If you know that your F[1] or D is generally on the flat side with the fingering you normally use for it, and you then find it is flatter than the other recorders you are playing with, you must either sharpen your instrument or persuade the other players to flatten.

Flattening a recorder is easily done by 'pulling out', that is, adjusting the main joint so that it is not quite home and the instrument is thereby lengthened. A quarter of an inch is the utmost practicable limit of pulling out as the effect is more marked on the notes of the lower octave than the upper and more pulling out causes poor intonation. The flattening effect of Plasticine 'wings' is a little more evenly distributed, and the device can be used to tune a recorder made in one piece (e.g. a sopranino). The wings are vertical extensions by about an inch of the side walls of the 'window' of the recorder with pieces of Plasticine rolled and flattened and pressed on each side of the 'window'. The 'wheel-barrow' sound-projecting device (see p. 102) has the same flattening effect. Both devices make tone more 'plummy'. This method of tuning is used with metal organ pipes which have two strips of metal standing out on either side of the mouth and at right-angles to the lip: if bent inwards they lower the pitch and if bent outwards they raise it.

A recorder may be sharpened evenly throughout its range, with only a slight coarsening of tone-quality, by the use of tuning holes. Two small holes of a sixteenth of an inch diameter may be bored in the side of the instrument at about a half to one inch lower down the instrument than the edge. Normally these holes are kept closed with wax (candle-wax is easy to apply and remove) or with a wooden stopper, but if it is desired to raise the pitch of the instrument one or both of the holes may be opened. Amateur carpentry on recorders may, however, cause damage, so such modifications are best carried out by an instrument-maker, preferably the maker of the instrument involved.

Beats and difference tones

Recorder players are lucky in that the 'pure-tone' quality of their instrument provides them with the assistance of audible 'beats' and 'difference-tones' to check intonation. Beats, which are most noticeable in two-part playing on high instruments, are caused when two recorders are not quite in unison: the beats become faster as the notes get more out of tune and when the two notes are a minor third apart the frequency of the beats has become great enough to form an actual note, or difference-tone, which should be in harmony with the notes producing it. Two descant players could, in theory, play a trio creating their own bass part in difference-tones, but they would have to play most consummately in tune—and there is no reason why they should not.

VIII

ALTERNATIVE FINGERINGS

It is common in the process of learning to become intoxicated with some new-found device, but excess leads to wisdom, and in more sober judgement the real value of the new piece of knowledge becomes evident. This happens with alternative fingerings on the recorder. The discovery of their existence opens up wide vistas of new possibilities of the instrument: fast passages that tangled the learner's clumsy fingers suddenly become easy; ugly slurs full of 'clicks' and 'in-between notes' become neat and smooth. New alternatives are discovered that make awkward bars into child's play. But then the player becomes more critical. Tonal inequalities in his alternative-fingered notes begin to make themselves heard, faults in intonation become apparent. He finds that the new facility in fingering which the use of alternatives has given him makes it quite easy to play previously hard passages with ordinary fingerings, which anyhow are more reliable under the strain of performance. And eventually he hits upon the paradox that alternative fingerings make the recorder harder to play, not easier. He uses them more sparingly but to far greater effect.

The diagrams on p. 70 for F^1 fingerings illustrate the principle of finding alternatives. Most notes of the F major scale are 'plain-fingered', in other words, working from the thumb down you have a number of holes all covered followed by the remainder of the holes all left open. F, G, A, C, D, and E are plain-fingered, while B♭ and F^1 are forked fingerings. Nearly every plain note has a forked alternative, but not necessarily perfectly in tune with it. Thus E can be played with the thumb and the first finger, or with the thumb and the second and third fingers; this latter is the best known of all alternative fingerings. Some of these forked alternatives can be 'double-forked' by lifting the lowest finger of the forked fingering and putting down fingers below it. Many forked fingerings can be widened by leaving two holes open and counteracting the sharpening by covering more holes lower down. An ordinary forked fingering can be so much flattened by adding fingers below that a note a semitone, a tone and possibly even a tone and a half below the original can be made to sound, so giving alternatives for other notes. Always remembering that a wide open thumb-hole constitutes a forked fingering, this principle works right up to C^1, above which forking sharpens a note instead of flattening it—consider, for example, the normal fingering for E^1. Alternative fingerings produce notes that vary to a greater or a less degree in intonation and tone-quality from notes produced by normal fingerings. Generally speaking, the more forked a note the poorer is its tone-quality and its capacity to react to stronger tonguings: even carefully controlled vibrato cannot disguise its tonal weakness. Forked fingerings over an open thumb-hole tend to coarseness.

The tonal differences between a plain note and an alternative are seldom so slight that they can be ignored. In the following uses of alternatives, therefore, these variations in tone-quality have either to be overlooked or exploited.

1. **Trills.** In trills and other rapid decorations the notes pass by so quickly that their tone-quality is hardly apparent. Neatness and shapeliness are the main factors. Good execution at speed can best be achieved by utilizing the minimum finger movements in passing from one note to another, and the employment of an alternative fingering can sometimes make the difference between moving five fingers or more and moving only one to change a note. This, then, is the most important use of alternative fingerings—indeed, they are often called 'trill-fingerings'. Sometimes the tonal inequality of the two notes of a trill adds interest and brilliance but care must be taken not to allow a preponderating note to spoil the pattern and fluency of a trill. Because a trill-fingering is generally forked, it is usually easy to add the turn at the end of the trill by putting down fingers below the fork: with normal fingerings trills with turns are often unmanageable. The forked fingering of a trill often makes the final turn, which would otherwise threaten to be a mess, very simple to play (usually two

fingers below). It is frequently unwise to begin, and, even worse, to end a trill in an alternative fingering position, for once the reverberations have ceased the possible poor quality of the note shows through. Quick thought matched by quick finger movements are necessary to get from the plain-fingered appoggiatura on to the alternative for the trill itself, and then off it for the closing note.

2. **Slurs.** Quick slurs often demand alternative fingerings for the same reason that trills do. Try the effect, for example, of slurring G¹ A¹ B♭¹ quickly with ordinary fingering and then with the usual alternatives for G¹ (all on except thumb) and A¹ (lift second right): one is inevitably clumsy and full of 'clicks', the other is—or should be—neat. But this slur in a slow, quiet movement cannot be alternatively fingered as the coarse quality of the G¹ followed by the much thinner A¹ spoils the evenness of the flow, and ordinary fingerings with their better tone-quality have to be used (see p. 85). Somewhere between adagio and allegro, varying according to the player's skill in tonguing (see p. 62) and his instrument's voicing and tone-quality, lies the point where the danger of perpetrating a 'click' matters more than the disadvantages of unequal tone, for in all slurs, and in particular wide slurs, the player must above all aim at a smooth transition—that is the composer's intention in marking a slur. Making 'clicks' over slurs is the recorder's equivalent of bad pedalling on the piano.

3. **Runs.** Slurred runs in quick music can seldom be played neatly without alternative fingerings: chromatic runs are nearly impossible without them (see p. 125). Moreover, a run which threatens to be uneven because of a difficult finger change immediately before an unaccented note can be made fluent and shapely by using an alternative fingering which throws the greatest finger movement on to an accented note. A good example is the D major scale played in the usual pattern of quaver, six semiquavers, crotchet. The accented note in this run is G¹: with normal fingering the greatest finger movement is from G¹ to A¹, which throws an accent on the A¹ and makes a 'click', but if the G¹ alternative is used the unavoidable five-finger movement is from F♯¹ to G¹ where the accent is needed.

Incidentally, the C♯¹ at the end of this slur can be played with the second finger of the right hand instead of the first so that a one-finger movement (lifting of third left) is substituted for the normal three-finger movement. Economy in finger movement is the main purpose in using alternative fingerings in fast music.

4. **Passage-work.** The playing of broken chords and other semiquaver passages in allegros is simplified by alternative fingerings. Particularly useful are fingerings such as F¹ with three left and no thumb (illustrated on p. 70), and G¹ with third left and first right only, as they can form a pivot around which other notes may be grouped. For instance, the common semiquaver groups A¹ F¹ C F¹ and G¹ E♭ B♭ E♭ are difficult to play rapidly with ordinary fingering, but with the alternatives mentioned they become easy because the fingers forming the alternative remain still for the whole group of notes, enabling movements higher and lower on the instrument to pivot round them with a sort of rocking motion: the finger(s) forming the 'fulcrum' should be held down firmly. This rocking effect is the secret of well-balanced passage-work. Intelligent fingering prepares the way to good interpretation.

5. **Intonation Control.** This use of alternative fingerings was dealt with in Chapter VII. A player should experiment with his instrument to find to what extent he may use alternative fingerings for intonation control without unduly affecting the evenness of the tone-quality produced.

6. **Decrescendos.** All alternative fingerings are forked fingerings; in the last chapter it was pointed out that forked fingerings are amenable to sharpening by slide-fingering. Conversely, such slide-fingerings may be used to keep intonation constant under a variable breath-pressure, so allowing a note to swell or die away (see p. 100). The latter effect is difficult to manage on plain-fingered notes and an alternative must generally be used, but once again with the proviso that it does not unduly change the tone-colour, or, if it does, that such a change is justified.

7. **Tone-quality changes.** The different timbre of alternative-fingered notes may be exploited to add to the range of expression of the recorder (see Chapter XI).

8. Keeping within the register. There are fingerings both with and without the pinched thumb-hole for A¹, Ab¹, and G¹ (and also F♯¹ but it is rather stifled). The timbre of the pinched notes matches that of the upper register, while the open notes have the fuller tone of the lower register. In playing a slurred adagio phrase that goes up or down to one of these notes it is as well to use the fingering that is least likely to make the note predominate by sounding different in quality. In fast music these notes are valuable to effect a smooth transition between the registers as the thumb may be brought into position while they are being played (as, for example, in the common G¹ A¹ B¹ slur).

In the following survey of alternative fingerings allowance must be made for differences between instruments: an alternative that works on one instrument will not necessarily do so on all others.

Alternative fingerings in the lower register

E: Officially the lowest note of the treble recorder is F. But, in private playing only, a low E can be faked by lowering the instrument against the knee so that the bottom opening of the instrument is shaded; the note should be played with little or no tonguing or it will sound F¹. This, with care, can be surprisingly convincing, so long as nobody is looking.

F: There are no alternatives for F. In order to play it pianissimo careful slide-fingering over the bottom half-hole must be resorted to, for it easily goes flat with lowering of breath-pressure.

F♯: Gb: No alternatives.

G: A rich-sounding note, slightly sharp on some recorders. If so, prefer reduction of breath-pressure to shading, as shading is of necessity very critical and coarsens tone-quality.

In trill Ab to G, G may be played 0 123 456̸7, without moving the right hand round to the half-hole position.

Ab: G♯: 0 123 45–7 with 6 heavily shaded may be used as the only alternative to half-holing on an instrument without double-holes.

A: A possible alternative is 0 123 45̸67: it is not much use.

B♭: A♯: Sharper (or softer) versions are 0 123 4–6̸7̸, 0 123 4–6–, 0 123 4–6̸7̸, and 0 123 4–6̸–. The latter is useful for the B♭ to A♭ trill.

Useless alternatives are 0 –23 4567 and 0 123̸ 4567.

A very slight lifting of 5 from the normal A fingering will give a poor B♭, virtually a semitone sharpening of A by slide-fingering. The right hand should be raised so that 5 is in an arched position and the curve of the finger-tip just touches the far side of the hole, leaving the near side open. Although the tone-quality of this note is weak and stifled, it is useful in fast trills from B♭ to A. The trilling finger continues to touch the recorder during this trill, moving on the elasticity of the fleshy finger-pad. Although the movement is so small it should be controlled and regular, otherwise poor intonation and blurring result. The recorder needs to be held firmly to negotiate this trill, so it is well to press hard with the other fingers and to steady the instrument by putting the little finger of the left hand underneath it, pressing upwards. Both this and the B to A trill (see below) tend to sharpness as it is difficult to keep the finger movement narrow enough.

B: The sharp alternative 0 123 –5–– may be used on the common B to A trill. Sharpening makes a trill more brilliant, but it is a trick that can become a vice. B to A trills can be more accurately negotiated with 4 moving in the same way as 5 does for the B♭ to A trill. It is by no means impossible to play this trill with normal fingerings.

The flat alternative 0 123 4––– is only to be used in very fast runs.

The poor-quality alternative 0 123̸ 4567 may be used for the turn after a D to C♯ trill.

C: 0 12– 4567 gives a wheezy alternative that does some service in the rare C♯ to B♯ trill (it occurs in a Bach flute sonata).

0 –23 456– is useless.

0 1–3 4567 may be used for the turn after an E♭ to D trill, but it is almost as awkward as ordinary fingering.

C♯: D♭: It is debatable whether the normal fingering for this note is 0 12– 45––, 0 12– 456–, or even 0 12– 456̸– (see p. 69).

For the turn after an E to D♯ trill 0 1-3 4567 may be used, and for the turn after an F¹ to E♭ trill 0 −23 45∅−: both these alternatives are too poor in quality for other uses. **D:** The most important alternative fingering to be dealt with so far is 0 1-3 45∅−, the 'one-and-a-half-below' alternative for D. This is used primarily in the E♭ to D trill and slur. It has a thin and remote quality that contrasts strongly with the powerful ordinary D, and as it is heavily forked it is amenable to slide-fingering and therefore to a decrescendo effect. This alternative is a little on the sharp side but as D is flat on some instruments by ordinary fingering the one-and-a-half-below fingering is invaluable for getting it in tune where a compensatory increase in breath-pressure would be undesirable.

The value of this fingering in the downward slur from E♭ may be demonstrated by playing the slur with the ordinary and then the alternative fingering: the transition from the subdued tone-quality of the forked E♭ to the firm ordinary D is ugly compared to the gentle sighing effect of the slur to the alternative D. For E♭ to D trills ∅ may remain down so that only 5 is trilling.

On some recorders the one-and-a-half-below D is too sharp to use, and the alternative must be fingered 0 1-3 456−. This makes the C turn after an E♭ to D trill easier.

Another useful D alternative is 0 −23 45−−. It is too heavily forked to be of good quality; its tone resembles that of the one-and-a-half-below alternative but is wheezier. It comes into its own on trills and fast slurs over the notes F¹−E−D, where the well-known 0 −23 −−−− alternative is used for E. Whenever the notes F¹−E−D−E are encountered in fast music, this fingering should be employed.

The D alternative − 123 45∅− is interesting but useless, and 0 −−3 4567 is only a tonguing exercise.

E♭: D♯: As the normal fingering of E♭ is forked it offers all sorts of variants: adding fingers below (7 variants) flattens it, while double-forking, e.g. 0 1-3 −−67, generally sharpens it. Because the ordinary fingering has a tendency to sharpness the most useful of this large group of alternatives is the flattening 0 1-3 4-6−.

A second group of nine possible alternatives is based on the important fingering 0 –23 4–––. This note has a reasonable tone-quality (though inferior to the ordinary fingering) and good intonation. It affords the best way of managing the common Fˡ to E♭ slur and trill (0 –23* 4–––), and the trill is easily turned by adding a finger (5) to give a D fingering already mentioned. Unfortunately the basic fingering of this group of alternatives is sometimes sharp and it must be flattened by adding a finger below such as 0 –23 4–6–. This makes the Fˡ to E♭ trill clumsy, and to avoid the three-finger trill one is forced to choose between trilling flat with 3, or sharp with 2. The trill can, however, be played with an Fˡ alternative followed by one of the first group of E♭ alternatives, e.g. 0 1*–3 4–6–, although this method may be criticized on the grounds that the upper note of a trill should, wherever possible, be a normal fingering, both to give the best tonal results and to make the trill easier to negotiate in the stress of performance. As it is quite impossible to trill neatly from Fˡ to E♭ with normal fingerings for both notes, the execution of this trill is a problem that every serious recorder player has to solve for himself.

A weaker E♭ alternative is – 123 45––. It is hard to see to what use it could be put other than in downward slurs from F♯ˡ or Gˡ, and such groupings as Gˡ–E♭–A are not usually met with in recorder music (they belong more to Richard Strauss).

The E♭ fingering – –23 456– is useless. It does, however, complete the pattern of alternatives. The first and biggest group of E♭ fingerings consists of forked flattenings of the note E; the second group are flattenings of Fˡ: the third is a flattening of the normal F♯ˡ, and the last of Gˡ. The more remote the original note is, the heavier the forking has to be, and, in consequence, the poorer in quality the alternative and the more difficult to tongue with the certainty of producing it cleanly.

E: The alternative 0 –23 –––– is so well known that it has been taken for the normal fingering of E. The plain-fingered 0 1–– –––– gives a richer note, however, and the fingering is easier to manipulate, particularly in the treble's

basic key of G major. The alternative, which is not perfectly in tune on all instruments, is most useful in F¹ to E
slurs and trills (with a 0 –23 45–– D turn), and it also
reduces the number of finger movements in slurs from the
upper octave such as C¹ to E. It may also be preferable to
the main fingering in the common G¹ to E slur, but this is
a matter of experiment and personal choice.

The flattening of F♯¹, already a forked fingering, gives
– 123 4––– as a fairly poor quality alternative E: it may
be sharp but can easily be flattened by further forking (with
further tonal damage). This alternative is of little use,
except as a possible F♯¹ to E trill as follows: – 123* 4–6–.

Almost useless E alternatives are 0 ––3 456– and
0 ––– 4567.

The two usual E fingerings, the plain fingering and the
0 –23 –––– alternative, seem to meet all exigencies, for
they are both amenable to intonation shifts on the principles
set out in Chapter VII. The plain fingering can be flattened
by wide forks such as 0 1–– 4–––, and the alternative may
be flattened in the same way or sharpened by double forks
such as 0 –2– 456–.

F¹: F¹ alternatives have already been discussed in some
detail (p. 70); if they were all counted it would not be
surprising to find that there were more than a hundred
possible fingerings for F¹ (allowing half-hole variants and
tonally useless alternatives).

The main alternative is – 123 ––––. It tends to sharpness whereas the normal fingering tends to flatness: it is
therefore very useful for dynamic purposes, particularly as
it is amenable to further sharpening. It is invaluable in
passage-work moving from the lower to the upper octave
across F¹ as it allows time for the thumb to move into place:
play rapidly C¹ F¹ C F¹ with both ordinary and alternative
fingerings to prove the value of the alternative (see also p.
77). This fingering should always be used to play E♯¹
partly because it is tonally weaker than the tonic F♯¹, partly
because it makes the F♯¹ to E♯¹ trill easy to negotiate with
–123 45–– as the D♯ turn.

The other important alternative, with a surprisingly
good tone-quality, is 0 ––3 4––– (sharpish) or 0 ––3 45––

(flattish), with 0 --3 4-6- as a variant. The latter fingering provides an F^I to E♭ trill already mentioned (under
E♭ above).

F^I may be played ∅ 1-- 45--, ∅ 1-- 4---, or
∅ 1-- ---- according to the amount of thumb opening.
This poor-quality alternative has obvious uses in quick
jumps or slurs from top F^{II}. There is a whole range of
'thumbed' alternatives in the lower register but their tone
is weak and intonation uncertain as the thumb position is
so critical.

A useless F^I alternative is 0 --- 4567: but it is interesting
because, contrary to expectations, sliding the little finger
across on to both its half-holes does not flatten the note but
causes it to 'break' upwards to F♯^{I}, a phenomenon peculiar
to the upper octave.

Alternative fingerings in the upper register

The exact position of the thumb makes or mars the production of good notes with alternative fingers in the upper
octave. To describe the movement of the thumb in its
octaving function it is preferable to use the word 'thumbing', rather than 'pinching' although the latter appears in
eighteenth-century tutors. This is partly to discourage the
taut and unrelaxed positioning of the thumb implied in the
word 'pinching' (some players press so hard against the
side of the thumb-hole that they actually bend their
thumb-nail), and partly to advocate the employment
of the method of octaving which involves drawing the
thumb slightly to one side from the closed position and
opening a crevice between the *flesh* of the thumb and the
rim of its hole instead of between the *thumb-nail* and the
rim as in 'pinching'. This method of octaving requires
the minimum of movement from the position in which the
thumb-hole is closed so long as the thumb is always kept
fairly upright (see p. 49). The thumb movement need be
no more than a pivot on the soft flesh of the thumb, a small
movement compared to the three-stage action of 'pinching'
(i.e. lifting the thumb, bending it, and inserting it into the
hole): the movements of 'pinching' can become so hectic
in a rapid piece of music that the thumb-nail misses its

objective altogether, with drastic results. Compare the ease with which rapid C to C^1 jumps can be managed by pivot thumbing with the awkwardness of alternately pinching and closing the thumb-hole. The one disadvantage of this method is that it is less easy to make the minute measurements of thumbing necessary for the perfect production of high notes (see Chapter IX) than it is with the thumb-nail. The ideal is a combination of the two methods, the thumb-nail being brought into use when accurate thumbing is called for on high notes.

Widening the thumb aperture in the upper octave causes sharpening of the note: with the thumbed $F\sharp^1$ (see below) the sharpening is considerable; with A^1, however, there is no such effect (a useful phenomenon); and with higher notes such as C^1 or $C\sharp^1$ the sharpening is limited by the breaking of the note when the aperture becomes too wide and ceases to have its octaving effect—within the bounds of safety, however the sharpening is sufficient to constitute an extremely valuable intonation control.

$F\sharp^1$: $G\flat^1$: The normal fingering – 12– – – – – is a forked flattening of G^1: it can itself be flattened by further forking, e.g. – 12– 45––, although with too many fingers added it may go down to F^1 or, surprisingly, break up to $A\flat^1$ (e.g. – 12– 456$\overline{7}$).

The note may be sharpened (for it often offends by flatness) by double-forking, e.g. – 1-3 4–––, or 0 1-3 –5-7: there are many variations.

The fork may be widened to give either sharper or flatter alternatives such as – –23 – – – – (sharper), or – –23 4–6(7) (flatter). The even wider fork – ––$\overline{3}$ 456– is a curiosity because it seems uncertain as to whether it wants to play $F\sharp$ or $A\flat^1$; its efforts at both are poor.

There is an alternative for $F\sharp^1$ with a truly vulgar tone-quality in 0 – –– – – – –. It is quite unsuitable for normal use but 0 1*–– – – – – gives a heroic $F\sharp^1$ to E trill on a D major cadence, although the alternative is so coarse that it must not be used even for a short appoggiatura before the trill.

0 –23 4567 as an $F\sharp^1$ alternative has only academic interest.

F♯¹ is the first note we have got to which responds to thumbing; the thumb aperture should be small: Ø 123 4567. It is mainly of academic interest, although it can be used for an F♯¹ turn after an A¹ to G¹ trill.

G¹: Like all notes in the middle of the recorder's compass G¹ can claim a vast number of fingerings, particularly as – ––– –––– gives a G¹ (very sharp and coarse). One finger on anywhere gives G¹ although – 1–– –––– is rather flat, and most combinations of two or three fingers also produce it—a veritable *embarras de richesse*. The only useful one of this huge group of alternatives is – ––3 4––– which is handy for the common E♭ to G¹ slur as it makes it a two-instead of a four-finger movement.

By far the most important G¹ alternative and the second in importance of all alternatives is – 123 4567. It is unfortunately rather coarse in tone-quality and must therefore be treated gently, but it is nevertheless indispensable for the trill A¹ to G¹ which is fingered – 123 45*67: it is the best way to play this common trill effectively, although – 123 456*7*, and Ø 123 456*7(*), are possibilities, the latter being useful when – 123 4–67 gives a sharp A¹. When this trill, as it often does, commences with an A¹ appoggiatura, the A¹ should be thumbed, for with an open thumb-hole it is coarse in quality and sometimes difficult to tongue; the thumb should be moved immediately the trill begins or the G¹ will be very flat. If the trill finishes with an F¹ or F♯¹ turn, the G¹ before the turn should be the normal fingering, and so, generally, should the G¹ after the turn. The semiquaver phrase (slurred) A¹–G¹–A¹–G¹–A¹–G¹–F¹–G¹, with the first two G¹s alternatives and the last two ordinary, should be practised to perfection (see p. 118).

On most recorders the upward slur from G¹ to A¹ tends to 'click' with normal fingering, and it is well to become accustomed to use the – 123 4567 G¹ alternative for this slur in almost all contexts. The only objection to its use is in slow music where the coarseness of the G¹ alternative may become noticeable and spoil a phrase by tonal ugliness or false accentuation: the solution is to tongue with such subtlety that an impression of slurring is given (see p. 62). The use of the G¹ alternative should be almost a reflex

action for G^I–A^I–B^I and G^I–A^I–$B\flat^I$ slurs, fingered
– 123 4567, – 123 45––, ∅ 123 –5––, and – 123 4567,
– 123 4–67, ∅ 123 4–6–, respectively, in each case the
thumb being moved into its octaving position during the
playing of the A^I. In slurred D major runs or scales (which
are frequent in recorder music) the G^I alternative should
always be used in the upward slur firstly because it facilitates
fingering, the first finger of the left hand being able to stay
down, secondly because the dangers of 'clicking' between
$F\sharp^I$ and alternative G^I are far less than between ordinary
G^I and A^I, and thirdly because the finger movement
favours the shape of the run (see under 'Runs', p. 76).
In F^I to G^I (alternative) slurs the likelihood of 'clicks' is
greater than in $F\sharp^I$ to G^I (alternative) slurs and fingering in
an F^I–G^I–A^I slur is therefore a matter of choice, dependent
upon the musical demands of the context and upon personal
taste. Rapid F^I–G^I–A^I slurs can easily be managed, almost
without 'clicks', by using an open thumb-hole alternative
for F^I, e.g. – 123 ––––, followed by – 123 4567 and – 123
45––. Downward slurs from A^I to G^I use the ordinary G^I
and never the alternative fingering (unless the slur goes
down and then up again).

The note G^I may be produced by the thumbed alternative
∅ 123 4567. As the tone-quality of this note is somewhat
stifled it is only useful in rapid music, and has to be used
with caution. Its value is in the mordent A^I–G^I–A^I, in a
G^I turn after a B^I to A^I trill, and in certain slurs and jumps
to high notes where neatness at speed can only be managed
if the thumb stays still.

$A\flat^I$: $G\sharp^I$: This note has two fingerings, analogous to the
main G^I alternative and to the thumbed version, each with
comparable tone-qualities. The ordinary fingering is
generally given as – –23 456–, or the same with the first
finger down (flatter and coarser). It will still strike on
most instruments without the second finger down (i.e.
– ––3 456–). Other possibilities are – –––– 4567 or
– –––– 4567 (both useless).

The sharpest alternative is – ––3 456–, and it is also the
coarsest. Even this, however, is on some instruments not
as sharp as it should be and an accurate $A\flat^I$ can only be

achieved by octaving the lower register fingering Ø 123 45Ø–, which then becomes the normal fingering. This note is true but comparatively subdued, its tonal kinship being with E♭¹ rather than G¹. It is easily flattened (little finger shading) or sharpened by slide-fingering.

Players who are fortunate enough to be able to use both the thumbed and the open A♭¹s may exercise their musicianship by suiting the fingering to the context. The easy sharpening of the thumbed A♭¹ makes it more suitable for use in quiet passages; while the open A♭¹ is used where accent is required. Jumps to the lower register are more easily managed with the thumbed fingering, particularly if the pivot method is used, but here again the context may require the more powerful note.

The A♭¹ to G trill is a crux in recorder playing. Here are twelve possibilities to try:

(i)	– 1 2 3	4*5 6 7	(A♭¹ rather flat).
(ii)	– 1*2 3	4*5 6 7	(accurate but difficult).
(iii)	– 1 2 3	4 5 6 7*	(A♭¹ rather flat).
(iv)	– 1*2 3	4 5 6 7*	(accurate but very difficult).
(v)	Ø 1 2 3	4 5 Ø 7*	(G rather sharp).
(vi)	– – 2*3*	4 5 6 –	(like the remainder, 'clickish').
(vii)	– – – 3*	4 5 6 –	
(viii)	– – 2 3*	4*5 6 –	(gives an F¹ turn with the thumb).
(ix)	– – – 3*	4 5 6 –	
(x)	– – – 3	4*5 6 –	
(xi)	– – – 3	4 5*6 –	
(xii)	– – – 3	4 5 6*–	(G rather flat).

A choice of evils lies before the recorder player: the first is to be favoured for very fast trills and the second where intonation becomes a consideration, while the ninth has a pleasing bright neatness admirable in some contexts.

The G♯¹ to F♯¹ trill is fingered – 123 4*5*6– or – 123* 4*56–, both being decidedly 'clickish'. Alternatively it can be played without 'clicks' with the fingering Ø 123 456*7, 6 trilling low as Ø 123 45–7 is a sharp G♯¹.

A¹: By a very short head, the best fingering for A¹ is the normal Ø 123 45––, but – 123 45–– and – –23 45–– are identical in intonation and only slightly less good in tone-quality, indeed so similar that except in slow music the thumb may be brought into the octaving position during the playing of the note. This characteristic is taken advantage of in the G¹–A¹–B¹ and G¹–A¹–B♭¹ slur fingerings already referred to, and it should be exploited whenever occasion demands so that the thumb can be carefully placed in the correct octaving position for the following notes (this is yet another good reason for always reading a few notes ahead of the note you are actually playing). Generally speaking the proximity of G¹s and F♯¹s calls for an open A¹ while higher notes and lower octave notes suggest the normal fingering for A¹, particularly if pivot thumbing is used for jumps from the low octave.

In the G¹–A¹–B♭¹ slur fingering the note A¹ is produced by the fingering – (or Ø) 123 4–67. This is a weaker fingering as it needs light tonguing and is a little coarse in quality with the thumb off. It is useful in the B¹ flat to A¹ trill, although one needs a supple little finger to keep it going long. A sharp B♭¹ to A¹ trill is Ø 123 45*––, but it can be brought into tune by trilling with 5 very low.

Another crux in recorder technique is how to negotiate the common slur F¹ to A¹. The only answer is to use normal fingering, pivot thumbing, and careful tonguing. At first the proposition – 123 –––– to – 123 45–– looks attractive, but in fact it is very 'clickish' and this fingering only comes into its own when applied, trumpet-like, to the slurred fanfare C¹–A¹–F¹–C–A–C–F¹–A¹–C¹, or, without upward slurring, to passage work (see above under the note F′). A slight increase in breath-pressure at the moment of the slur up to A¹ helps considerably, but it is agility of fingering that counts most.

B♭¹: A♯¹: This note needs to be played with careful control of breath-pressure as on some recorders it tends to blurt. It may be slightly sharpened by thumb movement or by slide-fingering (to which, as a forked fingering, it responds well), but the thumb should never be removed altogether for although the note does not 'break' it becomes extremely loud and coarse. Ø 123 4–67 gives a slightly sharp B♭¹ that is useful before the trill with A♭¹ Ø 123 45*6–. This is a more accurate trill than the coarse and sharp – 123 45*6–

fingering, which can, however, be mollified by a touch of thumbing.

A slur or trill from B♭ to A♯♭ is taken ∅ 123 –5ᵇ*– with 4 going down for the G♭ sharp turn. This A♯♭ fingering is tongueable but sharpish. The right hand should adopt the half-hole position for this alternative (see p. 50).

B♭: As with all forked fingerings, intonation control is easy to manage, quite apart from the use of the sharpening effect of widening the thumb crevice—at least to the point where the note 'breaks'.

The only alternative worth mentioning is ∅ 12– 45–– which can be used as a mordent or turn after C♯♭. In using it breath-pressure must drop slightly or it will strike E♭, for which it is, of course, the normal fingering.

C♭: When buying a recorder, one of the things that should be tested is the accuracy of the note C♭ with ordinary fingering and the widest practical thumbing aperture, for C♭ is a dictator among the notes of a recorder as it has virtually no alternatives and cannot therefore easily be sharpened. Slide-fingering is the only possible way and, as with all plain-fingered notes, it is a delicate operation. Flattening is of course straightforward, either by ordinary or by little-finger shading. The effect of the flattening ∅ 123 ––6– is fortunately slight enough to make a one-finger movement of the C♭ to B♭ trill: ∅ 123 4*–6–.

Mordents or trill turns after C♯♭ may be fingered ∅ 12– 4–6–, but this C♭ (or B♭ sharp) cannot be tongued.

C♯♭: D♭♭: This note requires at least two-thirds coverage of the thumb-hole, preferably an aperture equivalent to one-tenth or less of the area of the thumb-hole. Rapid repetitions require light tonguing and close thumbing. There is enough latitude of thumb-movement to effect some sharpening but as this note often tries to clear its throat before speaking it is wise to begin with close thumbing and the moment the note speaks to slip the thumb across to sharpen it—it should all be done so quickly that nobody notices.

A useful C♯♭ alternative in slurs (it is very difficult to tongue) is ∅ 12– –5––. This is handy for the common A♭–B♭–C♯♭–D♭ slur (or its reverse). As is to be expected of a wider fork this fingering for C♯$^|$ is slightly sharper than the normal fingering.

Ø 123 4567 is a sharp C♯$^|$ fingering useful in slurs down from E$^|$ to D♯$^|$. It is impossible to slur from D♯$^|$ to the slow-speaking normal C♯$^|$ without a violent 'click'.

We have now reached another turning point in the mechanics of the recorder, for contrary to expectations, adding fingers below C♯$^|$ fingerings results in an upward break instead of flattenings. This phenomenon is the basis of high note fingerings described in the next chapter.

'*Supporting finger technique*'

This method of fingering, also known as 'buttress-finger technique', consists of keeping the third finger of the right hand down for every possible note—it need in fact only be lifted for A, A$^|$, C♯$^|$, and a few others. It derives from the fingering of the one-keyed flute where the bottom hole, operated with a closed-standing key, is kept open for nearly every note, firstly in order to improve tone and secondly to steady the instrument. Eighteenth-century recorder tutors, including Hotteterre's 1707 tutor, advocated this form of fingering because it was felt a right-hand finger should touch the instrument to support it. Giesbert in his 1939 tutor (Schott, English translation 1957) teaches this fingering saying that it gives much-needed extra support to the instrument, facilitates jumps down to bottom F, and makes forked fingering (especially B and B♭) simpler to master. Experimentation with Giesbert's method reveals little to recommend it. With the third finger of the right hand down the interval between C and D becomes more than a tone on most instruments, and the pure quality of the plain-fingered notes is coarsened by the forking. Fingering in the upper octave becomes more complicated, and in the lower there is no simplification, for a movement of the whole hand, as in the interval C to B♭ or C to F, is easier to effect than the simultaneous movements of separated fingers. The argument about holding the instrument steadier is surely answered by the existence of the thumb-rest, which every instrument bigger than a descant ought to have; and, incidentally, extra difficulties are added to the already taxing task of turning over one's music if the right hand is hardly ever out of commission! Supporting finger technique is not to be recommended.

'German' fingering

On recorders constructed for 'German' fingering, B♭ is 0 123 4–––. This simplifies the diatonic scale of F major, but as B♮ becomes 0 123 ⁄4567 the simplification ends there. German fingering also runs into difficulties with C♯' (∅ 123 ⁄4567). This historically inaccurate method of fingering was evolved before the war to avoid a cross-fingered F on school descants, and became common in Germany. It is now moribund. Correct fingering is called 'Baroque' or 'English' fingering.

IX

HIGH NOTES

Readers who have developed the good habit of following this book recorder in hand should now shut windows and warn neighbours, for it is inevitable in introducing oneself to the highest notes on the recorder that loud and unpleasant noises are perpetrated before they become softer and sweeter through familiarity and a growing command of tonguing and thumbing.

Tonguing and thumbing—these are the clues to success in the highest register. Look back to Chapter VI and practise some of the exercises suggested there until the knack is learned of altering the degree of 'explosion' in the tonguing without changing the breath-pressure on the note itself. For application to high notes use a medium tonguing ('dh'), a strong tonguing ('d'), and a very strong tonguing ('t'): the intensity of the tonguing depends largely on how firmly the tongue is pressed on the teeth-ridge before the note is started. Using the note C^I practise these with the note played mezzoforte, piano, and as softly as possible. Obviously it is hardest to play the note very softly with a very strong tonguing, but although the effect may be odd it is worth mastering as a prelude to playing higher notes. The C^I fingering with a very strong tonguing and a high breath-pressure will, incidentally, play a sharp $A\flat^{II}$.

Now turn your attention to the thumb, still practising on the note C^I. As 'pinched' thumbing is more reliable than 'pivot' thumbing for high notes, first cut the nail fairly short. Place the thumb into its hole and, as relaxedly as possible, move the thumb about the hole, gently feeling its edges. Try pivoting on the thumb-nail so that the fleshy side of the thumb is lifted slightly away from the far side of the thumb-hole. All the while the thumb should be absolutely relaxed, and should touch the hole as if afraid to damage it in any way. Of course, if the thumb-hole is damaged or worn down by harsh thumbing it should be rebushed, preferably with ivory, for it is not easy to produce good high notes with a worn thumb-hole.

Apart from controlled tonguing and sensitive and relaxed thumbing there is another prerequisite to the successful playing of high notes. That is that the recorder should be dry. Drops of moisture in the tone-producing areas have a perverse effect on high notes, and as high notes generally take more breath than lower ones, conditions are conducive to wetness. It is therefore essential that for playing a piece containing high notes the recorder should be warm and dry (see p. 105).

In fingering all notes of the recorder, and particularly high notes, all the fingers, and indeed the whole hand, should be relaxed. Each finger should rest firmly but gently on its hole, lightly enough for an infinitesimal movement to be sufficient to make the difference between closing and just not quite closing the hole. Let us now proceed to the fingerings for each note.

D¹: This is not an easy note. Its normal fingering Ø 12– –––– requires no more than medium tonguing, otherwise it tends to overblow to a flat A¹¹. It is often flat, but may be sharpened by widening the thumb aperture immediately after striking; this sharpening device may be used on all high notes up to half-opening the thumb-hole. D¹ will only strike with a fairly small aperture—never less than eight-tenths closed, but on the other hand too close thumbing will make the note harsh, and tight pinching therefore spoils it.

A wheezy alternative for D¹ is Ø 123 4567, useful mainly for the trill after E♭¹. 3 should be about three-quarters shut controlling the intonation, and the trill should be executed with the third finger of the right hand (6). This fingering is also used with E¹ to D¹ trills with 67 doing the trilling. The alternative D¹ is very useful for turns after trills involving E¹. A coarser variant of it is to cover 7 entirely and make 3 only half shut; in this case the trilling finger for the E♭¹ to D¹ trill is 7.

E♭¹: D♯¹: The normal fingering, Ø 12– 456–, gives a clear and lovely note on most instruments. The thumbing is not critical—the note can be induced to strike with only three-tenths of the thumb-hole closed: the optimum thumbing is nine-tenths shut. For pianissimo playing the third finger of the right hand may be brought back to its half-hole: the note can be flattened by moving the little finger across to its half-hole.

Alternatives for $E\flat^I$ are $\emptyset$ 12- --6̷7̷, $\emptyset$ 12- --67 and $\emptyset$ 12- ---7, all of which can be used for trills to D^I, the last being the least 'clickish'. Another is $\emptyset$ 1-- 4567.

E^I is another easy high note with $\emptyset$ 12- 45-- as its standard fingering. It responds best to a strong tonguing and strikes at seven-tenths thumbing, the optimum being just over eight-tenths, a slightly wider aperture than the best D^I.

An alternative for slurs after D^I, and trills E^I to D^I (using normal fingering for the first E^I) is $\emptyset$ 1-- ----. In this fingering it is usually necessary for the thumbing to be as close and tight as possible, for the trilling finger (2) scarcely to leave the surface of the recorder, and for the breath-pressure to be no more than medium, otherwise—strange phenomenon!—the fingering may give F^{II} instead of E^I. A fast D^I–E^I–F^{II} slur is best played with this fingering for E^I as the 'click' between E^I and F^{II} is much less than the 'click' between D^I and E^I with normal fingerings.

F^{II} needs considerable care. Its normal fingering is $\emptyset$ 1-- 45-- and the optimum thumbing is nine-tenths. With this thumbing F^{II} may be played fairly softly. More than nine-tenths thumbing make a harsh F^{II}, so it is fallacy to teach that for top F^{II} the tightest possible thumbing should be used. With less than seven-tenths thumbing, F^{II} will not strike. The best tonguing is medium to strong—stronger than for D^I but not quite as strong as for E^I. Experiment with F^{II}s of different volume (although *mp* is about as soft as one can safely go), and gradually the note will present less terrors—and it is fear of the note that causes unrelaxed thumbing, over-tonguing, and disaster.

F^{II} is often flat, but fortunately it is amenable (more so than E^I) to sharpening by widening the thumb aperture. It can also be sharpened by a slight lifting of the first finger, and by the fingering $\emptyset$ 1-- 4--- with 5 shading.

Repetitions of F^{II} are difficult because the note is very

slow-speaking. A possible solution is to form the thumb
aperture on the side of the thumb-hole farthest from the
mouth; this may be done by pushing the thumb-nail hard
against the near side of the hole and bending the thumb
towards the mouth until it is eased away from the far side
of the hole. This method of creating the thumb aperture
results in quicker-speaking high notes, but it is harder to
control the extent of the opening.

F♯ll: G♭ll: This is the bugbear of recorder players. Fll
sharp is obtainable by a number of methods, but none of
them is entirely satisfactory. The best known is ∅ --- 45--;
this can seldom be coaxed to speak without sliding up to it
from Fll or Ell. Alternatively, Fll sharp will play on
∅ --- ---- in the slur from Dl. Slight shading with the
first finger assists the note, particularly if it has to be sus-
tained: thumbing is as for Fll. This note nearly always
suffers from flatness.

The other F♯ll is generally too sharp: it is fingered
∅ 123 4567, being easier to strike and pleasanter in tone-
quality, with 5 lifted fractionally from its hole. A way of
flattening it is to use the second finger as the octaving hole
instead of the thumb (both the first and second fingers can
do the thumb's work of creating an octaving aperture).
This makes the fingering 0 123 4567 with 2 and 5 'leaking'.
Such a fingering for F♯ll can be played quite softly and it
is then in tune. It is only a little sharp when played
mezzoforte.

A third method of getting F♯ll is to use the flattened Gll
just described and flatten it still further by shading the hole
in the foot of the recorder against the knee. Carefully done,
this is effective, but a little odd.

Carl Dolmetsch has constructed a recorder with an
'F♯ll key' incorporated in its foot section. It has a slightly
stifling effect on tone, but makes it possible to obtain a
perfect F♯ll and B♭ll. Such additional key-work could
also add a low E to the recorder's compass.

Gll: This note is gratifyingly easy to play with fingerings
based on ∅ 1-3 4-6-. Flatter variants are ∅ 1-3 4--7
or ∅ 1-3 4-67; sharper ∅ -23 4-67. Recorders differ as
to which Gll fingering they prefer—each player must

investigate the idiosyncrasies of his own instrument and find what suits it best. The tonguing and thumbing are the same as for E^I, that is to say, there is a fair amount of latitude.

Slurs involving G^{II} are difficult because it is too persistent to slur down to F^{II} without a considerable 'click'. There is no way out except to slur 'portamento' (see p. 62). The slur to F$\sharp$^{II} is easier with the $\emptyset$ 123 4567 fingering, but the semitone is rather a slender one, and where this slur appears a resourceful player would choose to use one of the sharper fingerings for G^{II}, giving a much more convincing G major scale, despite the inevitable click between F$\sharp$^{II} and E^I.

The short forceful thrust of air needed for a very high note can best be supplied by enunciating 'whoot'. This tonguing, however, can only be used when the high note is introductory to a phrase or if there is otherwise time to get the tongue into the 'whoot' position from its normal closed position at the finish of the preceding note.

A$\flat$^{II}: G$\sharp$^{II}: This note is fingered $\emptyset$ 1–3 – – –7, with the standard pattern of variants, and is best tongued very forcefully with a nine-tenths thumbing.

A^{II}: The fingering is $\emptyset$ –2– – – – –, and needs very strong tonguing and nine-tenths thumbing. This note appears at the end of the first movement of the Sonatina for treble recorder and piano, by P. Glanville-Hicks (Schott Ed. 10029). A^{II} is flat on many recorders but can be sharpened with slide-fingering.

B$\flat$^{II}: A noise somewhere near B$\flat$^{II}, but rather sharp, may be obtained by forcing a hurricane into the recorder with the fingering $\emptyset$ 123 4567 with 3 slightly lifted, or 'leaking'.

B^{II}: This is quite a good note, though always loud, with the fingering $\emptyset$ 12– 45– –, very strong tonguing and nine-tenths thumbing. It does not yet appear in genuine recorder music.

C^{II}: The normal fingering is $\emptyset$ 1– – 4– – –, but there are flatter variants. The thumbing is as for A^{II} or B^{II} and the tonguing even stronger: a sudden-jerked 'whoot' gives the best results. Breath-pressure must be very high. This note is used only once (by Telemann) in recorder music.

A veritable explosion of tonguing on $\emptyset$ –2– –56– will, with luck, produce the note F^{III}, but that is of acoustical rather than musical interest. A good bass recorder will, however, without offence to the ear, play a complete third octave up to F^{III}. The basic fingerings are:

$C\sharp^{II}$	$\emptyset$ 1-- 4---
D^{II}	$\emptyset$ 1-3 -56-
$E\flat^{II}$	$\emptyset$ --- -56-
E^{II}	$\emptyset$ -2- 4567
F^{III}	$\emptyset$ -2- -56-

The author's Stieber great bass (in C) plays $C\sharp^{II}$ with $\emptyset$ 123 4-67 with 5 shading, D^{II} with $\emptyset$ 1-3 4-6- (normal fingering), $E\flat^{II}$ $\emptyset$ 12- ---- with both fingers 'leaking', 1 more than 2, E^{II} $\emptyset$ 123 4567 with 3 and 4 'leaking', F^{II} $\emptyset$ 12- 45-7 and $F\sharp^{II}$ $\emptyset$ 12- 4--- with 2 'leaking'. There are higher notes, but those mentioned are all, if played accurately, good enough for serious musical purposes. To play successfully in this third octave demands mastery of shading and 'leaking'-finger techniques, or of other methods of partly covering the finger-holes by the required amounts.

There are yet higher notes than F^{III} for the aspiring mind with strong lungs and insensitive ears. But let us be satisfied with just one note in the fourth octave, a horrible G^{III} that can be made to shriek aloud in a tempest on the fingering $\emptyset$ 1-3 4567.

X

VOLUME

In his book *Woodwind Instruments and their History*, Anthony Baines writes, 'Should the treble recorder prove too soft for a modern festival orchestra, then let somebody remodel it to be louder, as has been done with every other woodwind instrument in the course of the last one hundred and fifty years' (p. 75). To say this is to misunderstand the recorder revival, for the recorder is mainly an historical instrument designed to re-create the sounds and style of the music written for it in days before large orchestras were common. Admittedly its incisive and melancholy timbre has appealed to some modern composers of chamber music, but even if its volume were amplified by acoustical or electrical means, (neither method being difficult to put into practice), or simply by plurality of players, it is doubtful whether it would be much of an asset to the standard range of orchestral tone. Moreover, any system of making the recorder louder or its working more efficient detracts from its historical genuineness. The recorder is by nature 'une flûte douce'.

The volume of a recorder varies with its voicing, its bore, and the material it is made of (see Chapter III). Moreover, different-sized recorders have different loudnesses. Sopranino and descant recorders are louder than trebles, tenors, and basses; this explains why there are few solo concertos for treble recorder, (and Telemann in his uses mainly the upper register up to A^{II}), but more for the descant, or, more exactly, the sixth-flute in D. But even the lower instruments can be made to penetrate a string ensemble if they are played with a full round tone which gives the impression of loudness because of its individuality: a tenor sounding well at its optimum breath-pressure at which all the breath put into it is translated into tone sounds louder than if it is blown harder to give a more forceful but less pure note.

Generally speaking, however, the simple rule for a

recorder player to make more noise is to blow harder. On a good recorder it is surprising what range of volume can be achieved without materially affecting intonation. It is a fortunate phenomenon that a note of constant frequency appears to become flatter as it becomes louder, an effect that can be demonstrated with the Third Programme tuning signal. Consequently, if a note increases in pitch and volume at the same time, its sharpening appears less than it actually is: in fact if the actual sharpening is slight the increase in volume may mask it altogether, and the note gives the impression of being constant in pitch. A solo wind-player is thus licensed to roam between certain limits of breath-pressure, and he need only begin to worry when he is noticeably becoming sharp or flat. He is furthermore aided by the accommodating nature of his listeners who, if he is carrying them with him, will be quite prepared to accept an A a quarter-tone out of tune if the melody and harmony seem to require an A and the player plays his note convincingly enough. A recorder player should use volume variations fearlessly to express the melody he is playing: he must listen that he does not go obviously out of tune, but if he gets worried about slight fluctuations in intonation, his audience will do so too, and both his attention and theirs will stray from the music itself and its meaning.

The demands of musical expression cannot be entirely satisfied in the volume-range contained within the limits just described, so a player must be free to blow at any breath-pressure he wishes, so long as good tone is maintained. In doing so he makes for himself an intonation problem, and must apply one of the intonation control techniques mentioned in Chapter VII. In a *ff* passage, therefore, every note is shaded, no finger rising more than a quarter of an inch from the instrument, with the lowest fingers actually covering their holes for most notes. In a *pp* passage the unused fingers are lifted clear of the instrument (but see p. 124), and most of the plain-fingered notes will be played with alternative fingerings, while notes normally forked will have the lowest component of the fork slid to one side or lifted altogether. It is excellent practice to play each note on the instrument *ff*, *mf*, and *pp* without changing pitch. The note C, for example, is heavily shaded for playing with maximum breath-pressure, and, as it is not amenable to slide-fingering, refingered for minimum breath-pressure, thus:

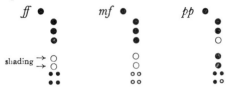

An even more valuable exercise is to do a gradual crescendo from pp to ff on each note of the recorder. A good note to start on is G^I; begin it with no fingers on at all, then as breath-pressure increases lower the second finger of the left hand to get normal fingering at mp, next begin to shade with the first finger, and finally add the little finger and the third finger of the right hand to their holes, with a bit of extra shading with the third finger of the left if the note has not by then broken: alternatively all the shading can be done by the first finger of the left hand if it is moved with extreme care. Similarly practise a decrescendo from ff to *niente*. When such dynamics are called for in recorder music it is best to get at once on to a forked fingering with its greater intonation control, and even the common diminuendo sign is a warning to begin the note with some shading. A difficult effect to learn is the sudden diminuendo following a rinforzando; only careful practice can synchronize the finger movement with the drop in breath-pressure. Extremes of volume variation should be mastered if a player is to feel confident in applying the more normal fluctuations which must be used to give even the simplest phrase its rise and fall. He should feel that each note is a being possessed of plasticity in pitch and intensity.

Although finger movements are the main factor in volume/intonation control on the recorder (unlike on most other wind instruments where the lips do this work), methods of blowing—quite apart from the basic fact of blowing harder or softer—can give the impression of volume variations. A note can be given prominence, for example, by playing it with vibrato, and, when a note is being played loud, vibrato has the double effect of improving its tone-quality and of preventing it from crossing the 'break' upwards.

An effect of variation in dynamics can be achieved by altering the attack accorded to a note (i.e. tonguing), and its duration. This method can be used on a small scale to shape a phrase, the more prominent notes being played with stronger tonguing and held on longer, or on a larger scale when whole passages are to be contrasted by the use of 'terraced' dynamics. When extremes of loudness and softness are sought, however, care must be taken not to injure rhythm, which is itself established mainly by tonguing and the comparative durations of notes (see p. 61). If, for example, three crotchets on the same note in a minuet bar are played with equally strong tonguing and are equally long (each note almost being slurred on to the next) the effect is of forceful, continual sound, and so of loudness, but the bar does not constitute a unit of rhythm as no one note is stressed more than another. Slight reductions in the attack on the second and third notes and in their duration (the third note being fractionally shorter and less strongly tongued than the second) provide the differentiation between the three notes necessary to define rhythm, while maintaining conditions in which nearly all the bar is filled with sound. At the other extreme, if an effect of quietness is required the first note may be played with light tonguing and a length equal, perhaps, to a quarter of the duration of the beat, while the second and third notes are played even shorter and slacker, the last just being touched as a pinpoint of sound: silence far exceeds sound in such a bar yet the forward movement of rhythm is still apparent. Recorder players must exploit such methods of obtaining gradations of volume as the natural volume range of their instrument is less than that of most other instruments. The possible volume variations in a bar where there are notes off the beats are legion, although in fast passages it is often sufficient to alter volume only at the on-beat notes, or even the first note of the bar. Experiment with a passage-work echo by shortening only the first of four semiquavers to get some volume reduction: then for greater contrast shorten all the notes in the echo, possibly keeping strong tonguing to achieve the dampened effect mentioned in Chapter VI (p. 63).

When a number of people play together small volume variations can be magnified into big ones, and the method of obtaining dynamics by altering the length of notes becomes more useful still, particularly as the breath-pressure method used outside narrow limits would only add to the intonation problems that already exist in consort playing. Changed dynamics in repeats can easily be managed by having fewer players to a part. When a recorder is playing with strings or key-board, the wider volume range of these other instruments can, by sensitive playing, assist the less richly endowed recorder. Subtle changes in speed and mood in consort playing can give the impression of more volume; if the music is exciting and intense it sounds louder, if it is calm and relaxed it sounds softer.

The recorder player should make the most of his instrument by choosing a position where the acoustics of the room will favour him most, e.g. in a corner which reflects sound. He should not put a screen immediately between himself and his audience in the shape of a sound-absorbing sonata perched high on a music stand.

Volume devices

Muting. It is possible to mute a recorder for quiet practice by covering all but the uppermost part of the 'window' with a piece of felt held in place with an elastic band. Another method is to put a piece of paper half in the voicing end of the windway, but this is a messy business when the paper gets wet.

Sound-projection. Volume can be concentrated into an area of a concert room by fitting projections above the walls of the 'window' which throw sound forward instead of allowing it to disperse sideways. This can be done by using Plasticine 'wings' (see p. 72), or with a special plastic attachment shaped like a wheel-barrow without a bottom which clips over the 'window' (obtainable from Dolmetsch). Secondary effects of these devices are that the pitch of the recorder is flattened, so encouraging compensatory higher breath-pressures, and that the 'breaking' point of notes, particularly those in the lower octave, is reached at a considerably higher breath-pressure. All this makes it possible to play the recorder louder, but not without making tone rather rasping.

'*Echo*' *key*. This consists of a tuning hole (see p. 72), bored so that its opening is in the base of the 'beak' of the recorder, and covered with a closed-standing key operated with the chin (a slight lifting of the player's head does the trick). When this hole is open, the pitch of the instrument is sharpened, or, conversely, it becomes possible to play much more quietly without flattening. In terms of pitch, the 'echo' key causes a sharpening of about a quarter-tone. As, with care, this key can be positioned between open and shut, it affords excellent volume and intonation control, making shading techniques look primitive. But then perhaps the recorder itself is somewhat of a primitive instrument. It was said of one recent harpsichord-maker who continually brought out improved instruments, that if he had gone on long enough he would have invented the piano. Are these unauthenticated sophistications in recorder-making a step towards the same madness? It is a point worth debating.

TONE

It seems paradoxical to suggest that the simple recorder is a more contrived instrument than the modern flute with its accumulation of keys, but this is true as far as that most basic of functions is concerned—tone-production. The recorder player has sound automatically made out of his blowing by the unalterable relationship between the shape of the windway which moulds to its own cross-section the column of air thrust into it, and of the 'edge' or 'lip' of the instrument which divides the air-stream and forms regularly alternating eddies which produce the vibrations of sound. The flute-player, in common with players of most other orchestral instruments, is able, within limits, to control tone-quality, but he has first to learn difficult techniques: the recorder player who, like the pianist, produces sound remotely, has the initial advantage of having no such techniques to master, but the ultimate disadvantage of not having much tonal variety at his disposal. He should, therefore, feel himself all the more obliged to study his instrument in order to produce the best tone it is capable of.

Achievement of optimum tone-quality

A recorder player should know enough about the construction of recorders and the types of tone-quality associated with different shapes of bore (see Chapter III) to judge what tone-quality the maker of his particular instrument had in mind for it to produce. A recorder with a sharply tapered bore cannot be made to lose its reedy quality for the purer, clearer sound of a more cylindrically bored instrument. He should, moreover, not mistake poverty of tone due to some fault caused by bad construction or poor maintenance of the instrument for an inherent characteristic. A breathy or edgy tone may well be the result of an instrument being dirty or in need of revoicing or rebushing. It is essential that no loose pieces of fluff or other matter should have collected at the sides of the windway opening opposite the edge or at the sides of the edge itself, and it is vital that the lower (chamfered) part of the windway opening should be absolutely clean and dry, and free from grease which encourages the formation of globules. The inner surface of the windway should be absolutely clean and smooth, as should the upper and lower surfaces immediately behind the edge. No loose splinters of wood should be allowed to remain in the bore, especially near and inside the holes. Joints should be snug and airtight and the plug secure (I have come across a brand-new recorder of an expensive make with a loose plug in the head-piece). Recorders have on occasion been sent back to the maker for revoicing when all they have needed is a good clean.

The finish of the recorder bore should be such that it encourages the gradual formation of a thin and even film of moisture during play. If this forms too profusely it makes droplets which run down the thumb-hole into the thumb-nail in a most uncomfortable way, or, even worse, block the windway. The recorder should therefore be warmed by a *dry* heat, preferably in the hands or a pocket or against a hot-water bottle at body temperature—more may damage the instruments (fires or radiators are generally too vigorous for recorder cooking). Blowing into a cold instrument to warm it up only encourages the thing that warming is intended to avoid, that is, rapid condensation of the moist breath in the form of globules on the cold surfaces of the windway, the edge, and the bore. The extraordinary but prevalent practice of 'blowing out' a choked-up recorder with a juicy spit into the windway only aggravates the situation. Once the mistake has been made and a recorder has been allowed to become wet, not just moist, the player must wipe it out, let it dry, and start again. A recorder gives of its best tone not when it is absolutely dry but when any unevenness in the resonance of the bore of the instrument is smoothed over by a thin film of moisture. To quote Bacon, 'a pipe a little moistened on the inside, but yet so as there be no drops left, maketh a more solemn sound, than if the pipe were dry, but yet with a sweet degree of sibilation or purling. The cause is, for that all things porous being superficially wet, and, as it were, between dry and wet, become a little more even and smooth, and if the body that createth the sound be clean and smooth, it maketh it sweeter'. (*Natural History*, cent. III §§229–30, adapted.)

The best made and the best kept recorder, played in a dry, warm room, needs skill and understanding before it will produce perfect tone throughout its range. The player must become aware which notes are weakest and, by concentrated experimentation and listening, should determine the exact breath-pressure required for the best possible sound of each note. Then should follow slow scales and pieces to accustom him to these tiny fluctuations of breath-pressure until they become reflexes conditioned by each particular instrument that is played upon. He will find that some notes are capable of producing stronger tone than others (e.g. G, G^l, and F^l), that certain notes are by nature coarse (e.g. A♭^{l} without thumb, and B♭^{l}) and some sweet (e.g. E♭^{l}), and that cross-fingered notes are poorer and fluffier proportionately to the extent of the cross-fingering. In fact, before long the player will find that every note has its own personality. This is one of the charms of the recorder—a wayward inequality of tone that it shares with a good counter-tenor voice, and which seems peculiarly suited to old music. Nevertheless, the recorder player must cultivate equality of tone as a prominent note in the wrong position can ruin a phrase. He must, therefore, be prepared to reduce breath-pressure on a strong-toned note so that it plays below its best tone and gives its neighbours the chance to be as or more important.

Variations in tone-quality

Flexibility of tone is a vital adjunct to variation of volume in achieving phrasing (that thing which transforms musical sound into music), and it is because so many players disregard both that the recorder is so often accused of producing an expressionless, emotionless monotone. The fact that the recorder has the smallest tonal range of woodwind instruments should be a challenge to its devotees to extract every drop of tonal variety their instruments will yield. The mechanics of putting breath into the instrument cannot, despite what has been said to the contrary, influence tone. Both old and modern writers suggest that tone can be improved by taking advantage of the resonance of the cavities of the head by stretching the soft palate and opening wide the gullet, or by constricting the throat slightly in the way a singer does: if this is true it is entirely psychological—the attitude of singing produces a more 'singing' tone. It has also been suggested that a thin stream of air projected with tightened throat or half-closed lips makes a different sound than a fuller stream, but experiment will prove that a constriction of the air-stream at the mouth-piece end of the windway has no effect on tone or even volume (provided the breath-pressure is constant); there is no analogy with the flute here (cf. A. Baines *Woodwind Instruments and their History*, p. 72), as the windway is long enough and the general breath-pressure used in the recorder low enough to allow the flow of wind to fill the windway before it reaches the tone-producing regions. The setting up of eddies in the air-stream before it reaches the edge by hindering its passage with the teeth and tongue—it is easy to fall into the bad habit of playing the recorder with one's teeth half-closed—does affect tone very slightly, because the disturbance in the air-flow makes a tiny scraping noise: this can be heard by closing and opening the teeth while playing a loud note, or by moving the tongue in the mouth to impinge upon the air-flow. The recorder should be played so that breath has a clear passage through the mouth—this may be assured by pushing the lips forward slightly in a 'pouting' position.

The only control breath has over tone is in breath-pressure. While it is true that each note gives its best sound at a certain optimum breath-pressure, some variation above and below that optimum will still make good sounds. The higher breath-pressures produce an impure, reedier, and slightly edgy sound which has the brilliance to compete with other instruments and is therefore suited to sonata playing, while the lower breath-pressures give a purer, duller, and rounder note of a more ethereal quality ideal for recorder consort music. Both overblowing, a common fault (particularly with descant players), and underblowing must be recognized and avoided, as the one causes coarseness of tone and the other a reticent breathiness. An overblown note is not the loudest note because it is not all pure sound, and an underblown note, though undeniably the softest, threatens not to be a musical note at all.

Rapid alternation of breath-pressures, that is, vibrato, is the recorder player's chief means of obtaining tonal variety. He should be able to play without vibrato, and with fast, medium, or slow vibratos of differing widths, and to move from one to the other at will, ranging from the calmest note to the most passionate. A phrase can be shaped by vibrato alone, the notes which it is desired to accentuate being accorded vibrato, while these in the trough of the phrase are given little or none. When variations in volume are combined with variations in tone, and the shape of the phrase becomes emphasized by the reedier and more prominent quality of the louder notes, the full expressive range of the recorder becomes apparent. As a general principle, vibrato is used on louder notes, which are usually the summit of phrases, and on long notes. A slight swelling of vibrato (i.e. making the beats of the vibrato slower and wider) adds interest to a long note and makes it more declamatory: this is particularly effective when a piece opens with a long note. Vibrato has the additional advantage of taking away some of the edginess of tone in a loud or high note. When the recorder is playing with louder instruments such as strings or piano, vibrato helps to give prominence to the recorder part. Slow music, which is the hardest to play, needs plenty of tonal variety, and it cannot be given full expression without carefully modulated vibrato to shape the phrasing. The slow movements of some modern sonatas, particularly those in a recitative style (e.g. in Murrill's Sonata), may be played with vibrato throughout, preferably produced deeply from the diaphragm to give a cantabile effect (probably more psychological than scientific). Throat vibrato, with its apparently lighter quality, may appropriately be used for music that is more instrumental in conception. The detailed application of vibrato and of volume variations to phrasing cannot be explained in words: it stems from musicianship, that quality partly inborn, partly bred of enthusiasm, self-criticism, study, and a sense of tradition.

Tonguing has relatively little effect on tone-quality, as it only affects the beginning of a note. A passage can be made to sound different by varying only the level of the tonguing, but the difference in sound is one of attack rather than of quality. Double-tonguing of semiquavers produces a slightly harder, more metallic effect than single tonguing, and strong tonguing at low breath-pressure on staccato notes a damped and spongy texture effective in certain contexts. Bad tonguing, of course, can ruin the tonal quality of a note: I have heard a whole passage of semi-quavers played with a spit effect at the beginning of each note due to too strong tonguing on the wrong consonant.

Fingering plays a surprisingly important part in achieving variety of tone. Differences in tone-quality are caused by differences in the intensity of the various overtones and subsidiary notes that go into the making up of any note. The breathy note just audible below thumbed notes on the recorder can coarsen tone-quality if the position of the thumb makes it discordant with the main note, and with two or more instruments playing discordant difference tones can produce a coarse and unpleasant sound. The cross-fingerings so often used as alternatives have a pattern of harmonics different from plain-fingered notes, and produce a less dominating, more constricted quality of sound extremely useful in soft, contemplative music when their comparative thinness of tone gives a pleasing effect of distance. In consort music these cross-fingerings are valuable in background parts when another player has the lead; they become essential if the notes in these parts are naturally rather prominent ones such as A on the descant, which in these circumstances would be fingered 0 1–3 456–. Other alternatives have a stronger and coarser tone than the normal fingering (e.g. treble alternative G^1: – 123 4567). These tonal variations of alternatives should be exploited in giving expression to music, as well as in avoiding obstacles to good expression sometimes inherent in the use of ordinary fingerings, for example the unwanted prominence of an

A♭^{I} in a C minor scale passage, or of an E$\sharp$ leading to an F$\sharp^I$, (better fingerings: ∅ 123 456–, and – 123 – – – – respectively). The demands of the music may require a thin and distant D instead of the firm and beefy tone of the normal D: the alternative provides it.

Even admitted defects of a recorder can be pressed into service when the context justifies it. The clicks made in changing registers sound very effective in a piece of sopranino bird-music (e.g. the A^I to G^I slurs in *Le Rossignol en Amour*) or for that rusty old clock in Britten's *Alpine Suite*, and the sharp trills a recorder sometimes tends to perpetrate (e.g. B♭ to A) have an arresting tone-quality most suitable in a virtuoso solo piece. Devices intended primarily to improve intonation and volume control also affect tone-quality. The 'wheel-barrow' sound-projecting gadget and Plasticine 'wings' make tone more penetrating and rasping, while the opening of tuning holes in the head-piece produces a very slight breathiness in tone-quality. Shading the foot of the instrument constricts tone and gives it acidity. The recorder built by Carl Dolmetsch with both an echo device operated by the chin and an F^{II} sharp key over the lower end of the instrument is capable of producing four kinds of tone on each note.

As recorders are not (at least in their smaller sizes), particularly expensive, players can widen the tone-colours at their disposal by the simple expedient of possessing two or more descant and treble instruments. The clarinet player, after all, possesses a B♭ and an A instrument for ease in managing various keys: why should the recorder player not take advantage of the great differences in the tone-qualities of instruments built on different principles, and possess a solo and a consort instrument? The former would be of conical bore and voiced to a high breath-pressure, so having a penetrating reedy sound capable of joining forces with key-board and strings, while the latter would be a more cylindrical bore instrument which, with a lower breath-pressure, produced a round and ethereal tone suited to the calm of consort music.

Given an instrument able to create beautiful sound, and a player with the technical knowledge to get it, there is only one more condition necessary for its production. And that is the right attitude of mind. No player will produce good tone unless he knows what he wants and believes in the goodness of his instrument and the worthwhileness of the music he is playing. Conviction will carry a recorder player far. If he truly believes that the instrument he plays is 'une flûte douce', the chances are that it will be so.

XII

ORNAMENTATION

Much of the best music written specifically for the recorder belongs to an age when ornamentation was an integral and essential part of music. It was an accepted convention that certain patterns of short notes should be written as one note, with or without an ornament sign above it, for decoration was so stereotyped that the context of a note was sufficient to instruct the player to execute a trill, shake, mordent, or an extended improvisation in the Corelli manner, as the occasion might demand. A recorder player who wants to do justice to the music he plays must steep himself in the tradition belonging to its period, its style, and its country of origin.

The complexity of the subject should not, however, terrify the player into disregarding it. There is a way to begin learning both the why and how of ornamentation, and it is the purpose of this chapter to indicate those beginnings so that a player knows and can execute confidently a small and basically correct group of ornaments which he can (and should) modify as he gains experience. The first essential in learning to ornament is to listen to as much sixteenth-, seventeenth-, and eighteenth-century music as time and opportunity allows—not just recorder music but music for all instruments and for voices. Even if it is impossible to undergo full-scale orientation by attending the Haslemere Festival or other live concerts of old music, radio programmes can always be listened to: many excellent chamber orchestras provide object-lessons in the style of old music. Knowledge of the social conditions of different periods and their attitude to the arts generally leads to a yet greater understanding of music. You will play a Handel sonata better if you come to it after browsing in the *Spectator*.

If you know what an ornament should sound like you will be in a better position to accept the guidance provided by editors of music. Some editions follow the admirable practice of writing out in full on a small stave over an

ornamented note the actual notes of the ornamentation
(e.g. Hinrichsen's edition of Telemann solo and trio
sonatas), while others put written-out ornamentations as
footnotes. One American edition (Music Press) prints
Couperin suites with written-out ornaments in the text but
the result is rather black, obscuring the melodic line of the
music and making it hard for the player to adopt his own
individual interpretation (within the rules). The same is
true of the 'grace-note' type of ornamentation guide used
in many of Carl Dolmetsch's editions. The most scholarly
approach is to quote when possible from the composer's
own writings on ornamentations, as Leonard Lefkovitch
does in Schott's publication of Hotteterre's 'Duo and
Rondeau'. In the early stages of learning follow the editor's
guidance: later on, when you have more experience, let
your own good taste be your guide.

It is not easy to lay down general rules as to when and
when not to ornament, as so much depends on the style of
the piece. Early eighteenth-century French music, which
is often not very melodious, depends for its effect on its
being performed with 'taste and propriety', in other words,
with appropriate ornamentation, and therefore demands
more frequent and prominent ornamenting than a piece
in the Italian style in which ornaments are less frequent and
more subservient to melody. The effect of ornamenting a
note is to draw attention to it: it has the same result as a
dynamic accent or as vibrato (which is a sort of ornament).
It should therefore be related to phrasing, decoration being
accorded only to those notes in a phrase which need stressing.
A secondary effect of an ornament, particularly one ending
with a turn, is to give music a forward impetus; this is
partly because part of every ornament is a discord and the
ear anticipates its resolution. The leading note of a cadence
is generally improved by decoration, and except in fast
pieces its decoration at the final cadence of a whole section
of music is obligatory. 'Embellishments', to quote C. P. E.
Bach, 'make music pleasing and awaken close attention';
the variety they lend to a repeated section of music, played
first only with cadential trills and such shakes and mordents
as are essential to the phrasing, is particularly delightful.

Rapid trills and flourishes have the effect of making music more exciting. This quality is both an advantage and a danger. It is good to be able to compel the attention of one's audience, but sheer pyrotechnics, which often sound much harder to execute than they are, can make nonsense of music. The criterion to adopt is, 'can each ornament be justified musically?' If there is no good reason to ornament, don't. Another general rule is 'never let ornamentation obscure the melodic line': if the tune is not hummable immediately after it has been played, it has been over-ornamented. Unless the style demands it, which is not often, ornaments should be played without accent, for they are accents in themselves. It is painful to hear ornaments thrust at one in the manner of Jack Horner's plum, or to have trills forced out up to the recorder's breaking point. In consort music in particular ornamentation should be, above all things, discreet.

Kinds of ornaments

To turn to the ornaments themselves, the most common ones are the shake, the mordent, the appoggiatura, the trill, the turn, the slide, the flourish, and the acciaccatura.

The *shake*, indicated by the sign ∿ , is a rapid movement from the note above the one that is written down to the written note, up again and then down again for the remainder of the length of the note, thus:

In words it goes 'Dee-er-ee-er . . .': the 'dee' comes on the beat, *never* before it. There should be a slight accent on the 'dee' (a discord) but normal breath-pressure should be resumed immediately afterwards otherwise the shake will sound forced. The *mordent* (∿) simply consists of a rapid drop to the note below and back again to the written note, thus:

It is a more arresting ornament than the shake and should not be 'pushed' in any way, although the effect of bite can be emphasized by making a tiny pause before playing the ornament. The 'note above' and the 'note below' refer to those in the diatonic scale of the piece, unless the composer has indicated otherwise by writing a small accidental above the decoration sign, or unless the note is governed by an accidental elsewhere in the bar.

The *appoggiatura* is a device for writing a discord in that musical shorthand known as figured bass. The accompanist in an eighteenth-century solo sonata was given only the treble note and the bass note with a figure below indicating the chord: to write the notes B, C upon a C minor chord, the bass fundamental C and the treble melody note C would have to appear to indicate the main chord, and the discordant B has therefore to be shown in small print in front of the C. Whatever note is used in the small print notation, an appoggiatura is generally equivalent in value to half the note that follows in common or duple time, and two-thirds in triple or dotted measures. As it is a discord it should always be slightly accented, and then slurred on to the following note.

The appoggiatura is not to modern ears an ornament at all, and it would not have been mentioned here were it not for its close association with the *trill*. A trill sign (*tr.*) often indicates that an appoggiatura must also be played, even if it is not written, except if the preceding note is the same as the appoggiatura would have been. In faster music, however, the appoggiatura is shortened, and in very fast music there is time only for the trill itself, although even in fast music some hint of an appoggiatura should be given at final cadences.

The trill itself should always be fast but neat, and the speed of all trills in one piece (or movement) should be the same. Although there is no such thing as a slow trill, trills in slower movements should be more leisurely and contemplative than the extrovert trills of fast movements. Long trills become slightly faster as they proceed (even though an editorial writing-out may show equal demisemiquavers), but the trilling finger must never get out of control and run away with itself—indeed the speed of trills in a piece is to some extent conditioned by the speed at which the player can manage the most difficult trill in it.

Unless begun on the note below the written note (see below), trills *always* begin on the upper auxiliary, i.e. the note above the one that is written, and should *always* begin on, and never before, the beat. If you feel yourself beginning trills early, cure it by deliberately starting the trill *after* the beat. The trill should be thought of as an extended shake (Dee-er-ee-er-Ee-er . . .), with a slight stress on the first note, a slighter on the fifth, even less on the ninth and none thereafter, as the pattern is lost sight of in the gradual acceleration of a long trill. In normal short trills the player should be aware of the number of notes he is playing, e.g. 6, 8, or 10, and the trill should remain even. It is important that the predominance of the upper auxiliary in the early part of a trill should not be lost by beginning the trill a demisemiquaver too soon after its appoggiatura— in other words when the appoggiatura is present (as it is generally) the trill itself begins just after the second beat, not on it. In an upward succession of trills the lower note is sounded first (as a semiquaver) and each trill is turned. This gives the effect of beginning the trill on the lower note (Der -ee-er-ee-er-or-er); this pattern may also be used for a trill on a note following a wide or otherwise dramatic interval, when to play the upper auxiliary first would damage the effect. Long trills or trills on the opening note of a phrase may be begun on the note below the note written (Or-er-ee-er-ee-er . . . er). J. S. Bach liked this decoration: he had a special sign for it (∿) and occasionally wrote it out in full.

Trills are of two kinds—those that end with a turn, and those that come to rest on the main note, then pause for a fraction of a second and finally give out one last short note that ushers in the next beat. The first of the following two examples, which shows a trill at a final cadence, is of the unturned kind: the second, a short passing trill, exemplifies the turned trill:—

It is quite impossible to legislate for turns at the end of trills, but these statements are more true than untrue:

(i) Passing trills (i.e. trills not at cadence) are turned when there is time.

(ii) Trills on off-beats (i.e. the 2nd or 4th beat of a four-four bar) are turned.

(iii) Trills resolving upwards are turned: those resolving downwards are not (see examples).

(iv) Long trills are turned.

(v) Most trills are turned.

The turn should be taken at the speed of the trill, except in passages of recitative or at the end of a cadenza where it may be part of a rallentando. A trill on the final note of a phrase has no appoggiatura and no turn: it should be short. In modern music, trills begin on the lower note except in pieces written in the style or form of old music, e.g. Herbert Murrill's Sonata (OUP).

The *turn* (∞) itself in isolation consists of four equal notes beginning on the one diatonically above that written, thus:

The *slide*, indicated by the sign / or written out in small notes, begins on the beat and usually consists of two or more semiquavers played rapidly to bridge an interval, often a sixth. The *flourish* is an extended slide moving up and down (above and below the note being decorated) within the diatonic notes of its chord; the turning points should be on notes belonging to that chord. It often takes the place of an appoggiatura in the final cadence of a piece and leads on to the cadential trill. Slides and flourishes are particularly effective in Sicilianas and other movements in triple or dotted time.

The *acciaccatura* is the modern grace note and should be shown as a small note with a diagonal line through it. It is played as quickly as possible and slurred on to its principal. It must not be confused with the appoggiatura, especially in the context of a quaver followed by two semiquavers, e.g.:

It is virtually unknown in old recorder music but players may meet it in arrangements of later eighteenth-century pieces.

A most valuable table of ornaments, quoted from writers of the fifteenth to mid-eighteenth centuries, is contained in Hildemarie Peter's book on the recorder (see p. 61).

Execution of ornaments

The best way to begin learning how to play ornaments is with the turned trill. Practise slowly the second trill on p. 117, first on the note D (i.e. E–D–E–D–E–D–C–D–E), then on F^{1} with the alternative E turn. Next try it on C, and top B^{1}. Now trill on E with the normal alternative for E and two fingers below that (and a slight drop in breath-pressure) for an alternative D turn. The A^{1} trill needs an alternative G^{1} turn and the thumbed one-and-a-half below G^{1} should be suitable. The other main G^{1} alternative (all on except thumb) is used for the G^{1} trill with A^{1}, its upper auxiliary, also being an alternative (– 123 4–67 —thumbed to start the trill), but for the note preceding the turn, the sixth in the sequence, an ordinary G^{1} must be used. This needs careful practising, but it must be mastered as the G^{1} trill is both frequent and hard to control, firstly because of the waywardness of the third finger and secondly because the tonal strength of the alternative G^1 tends to upset the pattern of the trill. A whole C major scale of trills has now been worked out, and it should be practised at ever-increasing speeds, though always kept neat and even and strictly *a tempo* (practise with a metronome if possible). The same exercise should now be carried out with fast six-note turned trills, and with longer trills of up to sixteen notes. Speed is essential.

When the C major trill scale is mastered, start at the beginning again with the A♭ major scale. Certain trills in this scale cause new difficulties. The B♭ to A♭ trill itself needs an alternative B♭ (0 123 4–♭7) to start it but as the trill with 5 and 7 is awkward, 7 may be abandoned causing the trill to be slightly sharp. This may be effective as the sharp trill has an acidity of tone that helps it to stand out, for like most low notes of the recorder it lacks brightness of tone, and the possibility of increasing volume is limited because of the low breaking-point of the forked fingering. If the context requires the trill to be accurate in intonation the 5th finger can still produce the trill alone by staying low over its hole while it trills, i.e. shading the B♭ of the trill. Similar conditions affect the difficult B♭ to A trill (see p. 79). Fingering problems arise literally at every turn, but experiment and reference to Chapter VIII should solve them. The general principles are:

(i) Whenever possible find a way of trilling with one finger; it is better to trill slightly out of tune with one finger than to fluff a trill with two.

(ii) If this is not possible keep the trill to the fingers of one hand.

(iii) Use an alternative for a turn even if it is a poor quality note and requires a drop in breath-pressure.

Trills should be executed with a hammering action and, unless there is need to shade the trilling hole, the trilling finger(s) should be lifted high between each blow: with light fingering, trills tend to speed up and run out of control. Although the trilling finger is somewhat tensed in its hammering movements, the other fingers should remain as relaxed as possible, all energy being concentrated, as it were, into the trilling finger. If difficulty is found in moving the thumb quickly enough to trill, hold the thumb stiff and shake the recorder up and down on to it with the right hand. For trills on half-holes (e.g. A to G$\sharp$) swing the whole hand round so that the trilling finger remains in a comfortable position rather than bent up (see p. 51).

Once the turned trill is thoroughly mastered, other ornamentation is simple if it is regarded as a part or as an extension of the turned trill. The cadential trill (as on p. 117) requires closest concentration: the appoggiatura should only be on an alternative fingering if the tone-quality of the alternative is good, so a rapid change in fingering is often needed for the trill itself. Similarly, the end note of the trill (i.e. the written note), should be good and not a weak alternative, for it is stressed and dwelt upon long enough for tone to be apparent. The final short note should always be very short and should be played with the 'gh' of double-tonguing: the pause for articulation before it should be longer or shorter according to the jerkiness or smoothness of the music. The mordent needs, perhaps, an even more vigorous hammer-blow of the fingers than trills. Slides and flourishes are, in effect, slurred scale passages; their practice is discussed in Chapter XIII.

This 'utility' guide to decoration provides the barest of furnishings. Once having mastered it the player must move on towards a closer understanding of music by studying well-edited publications, particularly of French music, and by reading. Particularly instructive are examples of written out decorations, cadenzas, divisions, extemporizations, and variations from the hands of composers of the seventeenth and eighteenth centuries. Every recorder player should digest Thurston Dart's book on *The Interpretation of Music* (London, 1954), and refer frequently to the two standard works on ornamentation, Arnold Dolmetsch's *The Interpretation of the Music of the 17th and 18th Centuries* (London, 1916), which is arranged under ornaments, and Dannreuther's *Musical Ornamentation* (London, 1893–5), arranged in chronological order of composers. These books may be supplemented by reference to reprints of the writings of musical theorists, especially Quantz's *Flute Tutor*, Couperin's *Method*, and the

'Embellishments' section of Carl Philipp Emanuel Bach's *Essay on the True Art of Playing Keyboard Instruments*, well translated by W. J. Mitchell (London, 1949). There is a useful book on Bach's ornaments by W. Emery (London, 1953), and the sections on 'Ornamentation' and 'Ornaments' in *Grove's Dictionary* are excellent. The study of ornamentation is so vast and fascinating that one can be beguiled into finding ornaments more interesting than the music they grace, but to fall into that trap is to commit a sin almost as great as the gross negligence of omitting ornaments altogether.

XIII

PRACTICE

It is difficult to know quite how seriously a recorder player should regard practice, and its concomitant bane, technical exercises. Unless the size of orchestras considerably diminishes (a development that would hardly receive the encouragement of the Musician's Union) the recorder cannot hope to re-establish itself as a permanent member of the symphony orchestra, and with its comparatively small compass and range of volume and tone—comparative at least to the violin, the clarinet, or the flute—it is unlikely to satisfy the tastes of habitués of the Palm Court or the local palais. Its status, therefore, will remain that of an amateur instrument. Amateurs generally have neither the time nor the incentive to spend long hours in regular practice, but on the other hand no self-respecting amateur could be satisfied with not being able to play music as he wants it to sound, and the only way of acquiring the technique upon which expression depends is by practice. Many players spend time simply playing through one piece of music after another: enjoyable though this may be it is less profitable in improving one's playing and understanding of music than systematic practice and concentrated work on a single composition, a process which eventually gives deeper enjoyment than aimless sight-reading.

An amateur recorder player's practice should arise mainly out of working at a selected piece of music and the desire to interpret it sensitively. Technical difficulties present themselves in almost any piece, for even apparently easy music becomes hard if perfection is aimed at. Hypercritical listening to one's own playing of a simple tune brings salutary realization of deficiencies in intonation, tone-quality, volume, variation and control of vibrato, while in more complicated music to these aspects of technique are added such considerations as unevenness of fingering in obstinate semiquaver passages, 'clicks' on slurs, and untidy ornamentation. So long as nothing short of the

highest standards is accepted, the preparation of a piece
of music for performance will reveal technical weaknesses,
and upon these practice should be based. It is a less
rigorous code of practice than would be followed by the
professional, but as enjoyment is the be-all and end-all of
amateur playing the improved playing of a chosen piece of
music is more satisfying than the drudgery of fundamental
practice with its less immediate results. The clue to success
in such a practice method is to choose for performance
only pieces which are well within one's capabilities.

Breathing and tonguing

A well-known oboe player due to play in the St. Matthew
Passion once asked to be provided with a studio for two
hours' practice: he spent the whole of this time playing one
note, over and over again, loud, soft, distant, commanding,
with all grades of vibrato from the plain statement of fact
to the most passionate and dramatic, notes which started
plain and soft and worked themselves up to a frenzy of
volume combined with wide, slow vibrato which narrowed
and speeded up until the note died away in quiet calm.
The chapters on breathing and volume (Chapters V and X)
show how practice of this sort can be planned. Long-note
practice gives the player the opportunity of knowing the
character of each separate note on his instrument—its
tone-quality and how it varies with differing breath-
pressures, the amount and kind of shading it needs at different volumes, and, in relation to other notes, its intonation
and how best it can be controlled (Chapters VII, X, and
XI). Its requirements of vibrato can be studied, for some
notes need a little vibrato to sweeten them even under the
relatively 'dead-pan' tonal conditions of consort playing.

The tonguing practice mentioned in Chapter VI of
playing B♭ with the fingering 0 –23 4567 is aimed at
encouraging light tonguing and it should be used regularly
as a reminder of what light tonguing is. Other exercises
are suggested in that chapter. Technical difficulties involving tonguing may arise from music with passage work,
with high notes, or, worst of all, with passage work on high
notes (as in the Second Brandenburg Concerto), where

tonguing, thumbing, and breath-pressure must be practised until all three are right on every note (Chapters VI and IX).

Fingering

Scale passages are so frequent in recorder music that the practising of scales out of context, although valuable, is not a necessity. Certain common sequences of notes, particularly those involving E♭ or B♭, tend to unevenness because of the disparity of finger movement; a three-finger move, especially if it contains the fingers of two hands or the sluggish third finger of the left hand (the finger that Schumann tried so disastrously to strengthen), tends to take longer than a one-finger move, and a one-finger move on a first finger can easily be skipped in a fast scale passage. 'Five-finger exercises' (from tonic to dominant and back) in keys such as F major, C minor, D major, A major, and F♯ major, help to even out awkward sequences: they should be played separated, portamento, and slurred. Purely physical exercises such as the independent moving up and down of those culprits the third fingers, or the sudden clenching and unclenching of the hand, spreading the fingers as wide as possible when unclenching and pressing them tight together when clenching, balance the strengths of the fingers. Softening the web between the fingers with olive oil and massaging the back of the hand between the knuckles also helps: if the fingers get tired with recorder playing, this rubbing, with the hand held absolutely limp, relieves tension. A player who habitually gets finger fatigue is almost certainly not relaxing his fingers and he should deliberately untense the finger muscles so that he becomes aware of the dead-weight of his finger-tips. When speed has been gained by hammer-blow fingering in the early stages, fingering should gradually become lighter and looser, though no less rapid in movement; eventually the fingers should rest so gently on their holes that the vibration of the air in the instrument is felt on the pads of the fingers. In the hammer-blow stage of learning to finger, the fingers must perforce be held high, but a practised player who holds unused fingers high is wasting effort in making his fingers travel farther than they need. If the fingers have

farther to move fingering is bound to be slower, so the ideal
to aim at is to hold unused fingers just above the point
where they begin to cause shading—if they are held too
low they may unwittingly flatten a note. As a general rule
the unused fingers should lie in a plateau about an inch
from their holes. The weight of the instrument should be
taken entirely by the right thumb against its thumb-rest.
The feeling in the fingers of a practised player should be of
buoyant lightness, rapidity and independence of movement, of fingers dancing over the instrument yet scarcely
touching it. Passages of semiquavers should trip along
gaily, the fingers lilting with the music.

Practice is the opportunity for experiment, and a player
faced with a difficult passage to master should see whether
it can be made easier by the use of alternative fingerings.
Where an alternative fingering is available, practice it until
you are familiar enough with it to make a fair judgement
as to whether it is better than the normal fingering: when the
difficulty is not significantly relieved by the use of the alternative, choose the normal fingering. The use of alternative
fingerings, especially in fast passage work, trills and turns,
and music where a wide dynamic range is called for, can
save a lot of unnecessary practice. Even apparently useless
alternatives may be pressed into service in certain contexts:
for example in extremely rapid slurs top or bottom B♭ may
be played unforked, or in trills from C to B♭ the first finger
of the right hand can do the trilling while the fork stays down.
The chromatic run in Lennox Berkeley's Sonatina can be
approached by using 0 –23 45–– for D, 0 –23 4––– for E♭,
and 0 –23 –––– for E, instead of spending effort on attempt-
ing to contrive a very rapid chromatic run in ordinary
fingerings. The principle to go on is to use the fewest possible
fingers for each note change: economy is the goal, though
false economy must be recognized and avoided.

Suggestions for the practice of trills and other ornaments
are given in Chapter XII.

Thumbing

Sudden jumps or slurs over wide intervals are difficult
on most instruments, and the recorder is no exception.

Success depends on the rapidity of thumb movement and control of breath-pressure (see Chapter IV and IX), and the secret is in the position of the thumb when it is closing its hole. It should then be so near to the octaving position that a fractional bending of the thumb-joint will bring it there: in fact the thumb-nail should touch or nearly touch the instrument even when the thumb-hole is closed. A little movement can be made quickly, a slightly increased stream of air put into the recorder, and a slur of an octave or more is accomplished with ease. The thumb must move quickly, but at the same time be completely relaxed. If it becomes tense with lack of confidence it cannot do its job so well.

All fingering and thumbing practice should be carried out to the accompaniment of a metronome.

Sight-reading

Apart from the technique of playing the instrument, the recorder player has to master the technique of reading music at different pitches and different clefs, otherwise he is not fully equipped for playing consort music. A treble player should be able to read at pitch (involving familiarity with ledger lines), and from music printed an octave lower—playing descant music on the treble is a good exercise in 'reading up' and in negotiating high notes: in consort music published with two viola parts the treble player may find himself having to read the alto clef an octave up, his bottom F being on the lowest line of the stave. A tenor player is frequently required to use a viola part, and he should also be able to read from the bass clef in close score. The bass player must be able to play from his usual bass clef and from treble clef both at pitch and an octave down when music arranged for that shrieking combination two descants and treble is made to sound more beautiful on two tenors and a bass: he must also be adept at choosing the right moment to move an octave up when notes lower than F are looming in his score. Recorder players may at least be thankful that the French violin clef is no longer in use. Some musicians evolve fascinating short cuts to cope with different clefs, but for the recorder player the best way of approaching a strange clef is to locate two or three notes to act as 'anchors' and then to read by intervals as a singer does. Thus a tenor player reading the alto clef locates G, C¹, and G¹: the piece starts on D¹, goes up by a third, then down a fourth, when the player checks he is playing C¹ (middle line). Common accidentals such as B♭ and F♯ also assist the player in finding his way around. An excellent exercise is to sing the piece to the names of the notes. This 'interval' method is better than any 'mechanical' process of reading, because the player must hear the interval in his mind, and this 'pre-hearing' of sound—knowing in advance the note, or sequence of notes, which must be produced—is the secret of good sight-reading. In sight-reading practice, deliberately keep the eyes ahead of the notes that are being played, and if they slip back force them forward again. Get a friend un-expectedly to snatch the music away from you while you are playing and see how far you can go on without it. The ability to read well ahead makes awkward turn-overs more manageable.

Take every opportunity of combining practice with pleasure. Use good music as your basis of practice: if you exhaust the technical difficulties in Handel and Telemann (and you will be a good player to do that) appropriate Bach's flute sonatas as recorder music, for the remoter keys—one movement is in C♯ minor—offer all sorts of new difficulties. Country dance tunes, and especially those from Ireland and Scotland, provide excellent material for finger exercises, and compel one to maintain a firm rhythm at the same time. To test the efficacy of your practice play the recorder for some country dance society—extra musicians are generally welcomed. Above all, be purpose-ful. The singling out of imperfections and their systematic elimination is the only way to progress. Your private practice should be such that if at any time someone inter-rupted you and asked to what purpose you were practising, you could give a cogent and unashamed answer.

XIV

PERFORMANCE

Performance is not necessarily public, nor indeed need there be an audience at all. It is an attitude of mind, the putting over of the finished product. There are three stages in playing music—reading, rehearsal, and performance. Reading is the process of familiarization when an attempt is made to hear the music as a whole and to find what it is about; rehearsal is the section by section analysis of the music when decisions are reached on details of interpretation and how this interpretation may be expressed in terms of the technical potentialities of the instruments being used; performance is the final result, the exhibiting of music to a real or imagined audience. In performing music the player is more emotionally alert to the music, for by then the reason for every turn of phrase and its relation to the meaning of the piece as a whole will have been worked out: in performance the players' understanding becomes the audience's experience.

In choosing music for performance it is important, therefore, to select a piece that is within one's understanding, and not of such difficulty that that understanding cannot truly be expressed. In fact, as far as technical difficulty is concerned, the music chosen should be such that the player regards it as 'easy' (a standard of difficulty varying with his technical proficiency); then his mind will not be distracted by questions of technique when he is actually performing the piece. The music chosen should be a piece the player likes well enough for him to want other people to hear and like it. It should also be one which, if there is a real audience, is likely to appeal to the tastes of that audience—their best tastes. One would not, for example, present a programme of In Nomines to an audience of school-children.

Preparation of music for performance

There is a definite order in which the preparation of music for performance should be carried out.

Style. First read the music (not necessarily playing it) to discover what it is about. Unless it is 'programme' music its real meaning will be in musical terms, but some attempt at extra-musical categorizing should be attempted. Most music, for example, falls into one of the three categories of song, dance, or narration. If the music is song-like, that is to say amenable to a verse pattern of words and containing relatively few wide intervals, a clue to its interpretation is already given—it should imitate the flexible movement of poetry with groups of notes articulating the syllables of individual words. If the music is intended to accompany dance, or is in a dance form, it should be related to the steps of the dance—certain notes should be played much shorter than their written value to give 'lift' and the rhythm should be deliberate and forward-moving so that it carries the dancers with it: in this connexion it is important to know something about the steps of old dances (see Mabel Dolmetsch's two books. *The Dances of England and France* and *The Dances of Spain and Italy*, London, 1949 and 1954). If the music is in an extended narrative form, it must be thought of as a complex of words, sentences, and paragraphs, of statements developed and carried to a conclusion. Music may easily have elements of each of these categories, but, more often than not, one predominates. A second method of approach to music is to discover its prevailing mood; one should be receptive to any emotion it might express, or to a 'programme' or series of pictures or events it might suggest, for imagination engenders feeling, and to feel something about a piece of music leads to good phrasing. External indications such as the composer's title of a piece, or its context in, say, a cantata or an opera, provide a valuable guide to the mood of a piece of music. Music can further be categorized by its period and its style. If a piece of eighteenth-century music can be recognized as, say, an overture in the French style, the player who (as every recorder player should) has listened to and read about the music of that time knows at once how to play it: dotted notes are held on, semiquavers shortened and double-tongued, the movement made slow and lurching, and the sonority excited and pageant-like. To know about music and, before playing a note, to think systematically about each piece that is to be performed, is the secret of playing it well.

The next stage in one's train of thought is to consider the *speed* of the piece. If the music is in dance form the steps of the dance may decide the speed (although some dances such as the Saraband varied in speed between different periods): if the music is song-like it cannot be too fast for the proper articulation and expression of words. The time-signature taken in conjunction with the sometimes mis-leading Italian speed indication (Allegro, Largo, etc.) and with the nature and frequency of the shortest-value note in the piece supply the remaining objective guidance (Fritz Rothschild's book on *The Lost Tradition in Music* (London, 1953) is interesting to read on this subject). It must be remembered that in old music fast movements were slower and slow movements faster than in more recent music. Pro-vided one is equipped to judge, one's own feeling as to how fast a piece should be matters more than anything, but even this should be modified by considerations as to how quickly, or slowly, one can play the piece, although if there is a noteworthy difference between the manageable speed and the ideal speed, the piece should be regarded as too difficult for present performance. When the speed of a piece has been decided upon, it should be found on the metronome and marked down on the score for further reference. In the latter stages of rehearsal the whole piece should be played through once or twice with the metronome going: this can be an interesting and salutary experience.

Phrasing should now be thought about and the conse-quential breath-marks pencilled in. Breath-marks may be made with curved ticks, thus ✓ , the size of the tick varying with the size of the breath. Phrasing marks where no breath need be taken should be made with a comma. In consort music entries should be marked thus ▭ , the thickness of the lines varying with the importance of the entries. Phrasing is dependent upon form. First of all, then, the player must examine the structure of the piece and mark it out into sections. In a sonata these will be statement, development, recapitulation, coda, etc.; in a rondo they will be theme and episodes; in a chaconne each section will

be the length of the ground-bass motif; in a fancy the
emergence of each new theme to be worked on marks the
beginning of each section, generally overlapping the previous
section. Even if a piece has no obvious sections into which
it can be broken up (double-bars, etc.), a count of the total
number of bars and their division by two, three, or four
will probably reveal that the piece is, in fact, made up of
sections with the same number of bars, usually eight,
twelve, or sixteen. Each of these sections should be marked
off lightly with a big breath-mark, unless a double-bar, a
change of key or a long rest makes it superfluous. The
'half-way mark' should next be looked for, and a slightly
smaller breath-mark lightly pencilled in. When this
mathematical process has brought one down to sub-sections
of four, six, or eight bars, the shape of the opening theme
should be examined, and any modification of sectional
breath-marks made according to whether it starts on,
before, or just after the bar, for generally the position in the
bar at which the opening statement starts conditions the
phrasing throughout the piece. Next, one must find where
the first phrase ends: if this is not evident, it may be revealed
by accompanying harmonies, or deduced from the treatment
of the phrase later in the piece or in other parts. Once the
opening phrase, the germ of the whole piece, has been ascer-
tained, its enunciation should be marked down either by
staccato, stress, and slur marks, or by writing over it a pattern
of words that will serve as a permanent reminder of its nature.
A mixture of mathematics, reasoning by analogy, and good
taste will decide the positions of all other breath-marks that
might be needed. If the music is fast breath-marks may be
too far apart to mark all phrasing, so commas should then be
used, following the same principles. In preparing for performance nothing should be left to be dealt with *ex tempore*:
performances which sound the most spontaneous are those
which have been most carefully prepared.

Particular attention must be paid to phrasing in consort
music. This is partly because phrases in consort music
overlap, partly because their ends are indefinite. Players
must decide between themselves when their part becomes
less important than someone else's: a good way of preparing

a consort piece is to go through it with only the preponderating part playing, the theme being thrown from
one player to another. Another approach is for every
player to play each part in turn, as if in a round. In Italian
and English consort music in particular, one should expect
to find breath-marks occurring between notes of the same
pitch, between two short notes, or between a dotted note
and the following short note: phrasing on the beat is more
often wrong than right. Players of consort music must
depend more on analogy and less on mathematics.

Unless there is a rest, the time taken by breathing must
come out of the note before the breath-mark. The player
must decide exactly how much time he can afford to give
to each breath. If he takes too long he might spoil a phrase
by cutting the last note short or even endanger a chord: on
the other hand if he does not inhale enough air he might
spoil the following phrase. He must, therefore, make
allowance for frequent breathing, particularly as under the
nervous conditions of performance he will need more breath
than in rehearsal. In rehearsal, therefore, the lungs must
always feel comparatively full: if they do not, more breath-
marks should be made in the music. Very long notes constitute a problem. If there are two or more players to a
part arrangements can be made to breathe at different
times during the note. Otherwise, the player must take a
good lungful of air and, using as low a breath-pressure as
possible, hope he lasts it out: it is better to break a long note
to breathe rather than to peter out in ignominy just before
the end. Extended passages of semiquavers are also
difficult: a solution is to leave out an occasional note, choosing those that are off the beat, that belong to the chord of
the harmony, and that come at the end of decrescendos.
The note(s) to be omitted should be ringed and a breath-
mark put above. If a recorder is playing with strings or
keyboard, the other players should know where breaths
are being taken and make the necessary allowances in time
and phrasing: if the other players are accompanying a
recorder, they should breathe with the soloist, lifting their
bows or hands at the phrase marks.

Dynamics. If the editor has not already done so, go

through the music marking volume indications, working on the principles that no repeat passage is played exactly the same way the second time as the first. In eighteenth-century music echos should be looked for and marked as such; in consort music each new theme should be announced in such a way that it sounds new—louder, softer, smoother, sprightlier, etc. In sets of variations or chaconnes each section should have its own dynamic level. When more than one player is taking each part dynamic variations can be achieved by arranging for fewer people to play in the softer passages; if this is done the instructions to the players should be indicated on the music in the preparation stage—'soli' and 'tutti' or something more complicated.

Ornamentation. First, is ornamentation needed at all? If it is, which ornaments are obligatory, which optional? It might be well to play only the obligatory ornaments—cadential trills, etc.—at the first playing and to decorate more lavishly for the repeat. In this case obligatory ornament might be marked in ink, optional ones in pencil. Every ornament should be marked down and nothing should be deliberately left to improvisation, even though some improvisations might be generated in the heat of performance. The length of appoggiaturas should be noted, especially when two players are trilling together, and for true precision the number of notes in each trill should be settled, unless the trill is a long one. Turned trills should be indicated with a pair of semiquavers showing the turn (the eighteenth-century convention). Pick out and practise the most difficult trills in the piece to bring them up to speed. Passages that are heavily ornamented should be played through with the metronome to ensure that ornaments begin on, and not before, the beat.

Alternative fingerings should be marked with a cross: failure to do so could easily cause a player to be left in panicky indecision with his fingers fluttering ineffectually. Unusual alternative fingerings might be written out in a memorandum at the bottom of the page. *Vibrato* may be marked with a wavy line the undulations of which correspond to the width and the 'wave-length' of the vibrato, and *shading* or slide-fingering with a downward or upward

line the slope of which denotes the extent of the shading or
sliding required. In a *ff* or crescendo passage when shading
might be applied over a number of notes the shading line
should be extended, sloping farther down as more shading
is applied, and the word 'shade' marked in. Editorial
phrase-marks or ill-judged slurs that clash with one's own
interpretation of the piece may need crossing out or
altering. All such markings should be made in pencil,
otherwise the technical commentary on the music could
easily obscure the notes themselves. Of all the technical
apparatus that appears on a thoroughly prepared piece of
music, however, nothing matters so much as those two or
three guiding adjectives at the beginning of the piece that
remind the player how the piece is to be played as a whole.

Leading. Understanding should be reached before performance on such important details as to who is going to
give the lead to start a piece, and who should be watched for
the finishing of closing notes (usually but not always the
player of the top part); the leader can indicate the tempo of
a piece by raising his instrument in time with the beat preceding the start of the music, or he can count out one or
more beats with the unused little finger of the left hand. Before
beginning the leader should catch the eyes of all the other
players to see that they are ready to start, and are not taken
unawares with empty lungs right at the beginning of a piece.
Music should be marked as to who is giving a lead and an ending, and when two or more players are sharing a piece of music,
who is going to turn over the pages. It should be clearly
written on the music when repeats are not to be observed.

Final preparation for performance

When the music is prepared, the instrument itself should
be looked at. Make sure that the windway is clear from
dirt or fluff and that the bore is clean and dry. See that the
foot-joint is in the most comfortable position for the little
finger. If a piano is being used tune to its pitch before
appearing for performance: a consort of recorders should
know how far, if at all, each recorder has to be pulled
out to be in tune. Recorders should all be warm before

performance, and if more than one is to be used a table in a warm place in the room should be available: the head joints of instruments which are to be most played on (or in the case of the bass, the crook) should be kept in one's pocket when not being used. If the recorder is warm, clean, and dry, nothing at all need be done before performance, except perhaps to tune with strings. It is possible that the room in which the performance is to take place cannot be as warm as it ought to be, or the atmosphere might be humid: in this case to avoid condensation the player must play as dryly as possible, using a slightly lower breath-pressure and avoiding drinking soon before playing. To take a sea-sickness tablet of the type that lessens the flow of saliva is a good insurance against clogging. Choose to play in the corner of a room from which the sound can be thrown forward, but if a piano is being used for accompaniment be near to it. For good ensemble players should be as near to each other as is convenient, and should arrange themselves in the order of the parts they are playing—descant next to treble, treble next to tenor, and so on. Every player should be able to see every other player. Music-stands should not be used as barriers between player and audience. The recorder can be played equally well whether the player is standing or sitting: the only considerations are comfort, and effect. For solo sonatas one normally stands up—the effect is better on the audience, but consort music looks more comfortable seated. If you have a few moments to spare before the actual performance, spend them looking at the first piece of music you have to play, and all the while keep moving the third finger of each hand up and down on their holes—this helps to ensure fluency and independence of finger movement. Remind your feet not to beat time.

All is now ready, and the point is reached where the players, for those few brief seconds, look at the music before them, hear in their minds the sound of the opening bars played at their right speed and style, then set in motion that inward rhythm that is to govern the piece, and, picking up its imperturbable beat, begin. Now let the music carry you forward: subject yourself to it, and forget technique.

51432

0428

SOME RECORDERS AVAILABLE IN THE UNITED KINGDOM

This summary of recorders available (January 1969) through London agents is intended as a guide to recorder players, but the following points should be noted:

1. The list does not claim to be complete; agencies (given in brackets in the list) sometimes change, new makes and models come on the market, and others are withdrawn.
2. The opinions are those of the writer; one man's recorder is another man's poison.
3. Not all sizes and qualities of the makes of recorder mentioned were available for testing by the writer.
4. The examples played may not be representative of the type as a whole. Recorders vary considerably, particularly high-quality 'hand-made' recorders, each one of which has a personality of its own.
5. Recorders respond differently to different people's ways of playing.
6. New recorders differ less than those which have been played on for some time, indeed some cheap recorders may sound better when new than more expensive recorders. Expensive recorders made in very hard woods, however, will last longer (though they are also more liable to develop cracks if not carefully looked after).
7. Not all recorders are at British Standard pitch (Dolmetsch, Küng, Moeck and Schott all conform), nor do all comply with the standards of construction laid down by the British Standards Institute—the 'kite-mark' reference is B.S. 3499: Part 2A:1964 Recorders.

ADLER (Dallas Arbiter, Clifton Street, London, E.C.2)

Adler recorders (Descant, Treble, and Tenor) are made in five quality ranges: 'School', 'Solo', and three kinds of 'Barockmeister'. The School and Solo recorders are built to the same general design but the Solo has a better finish: they have a powerful and edgy tone favouring the lower register, and a quick and vigorous response, with good intonation. The Barockmeister recorders, which may be obtained with ivory garnishings, are in a high price range; they are made of impregnated woods, have a narrower bore, and produce a clear, creamy and rather refined tone, excellent in the upper register above the F$\sharp^1$ G$\sharp^1$ level (treble). The descant

Barockmeister has a very reedy tone. The Solo tenor recorders may be picked out as being of particularly good value.

Adler make good one-piece sopraninos, and basses both on the 'Knick' system (see p. 38) and in the normal bassoon style. The Knick-system bass is easy to handle and is responsive to a wide range of breath-pressures: four holes are operated with keys. Some modification of normal fingerings is needed in the upper register for good intonation. Adler also make great bass recorders.

BOOSEY AND HAWKES (295 Regent Street, London, W.1)

This firm produces a range of inexpensive pearwood recorders: their tone is clear and round (though rather small), well suited to consort playing.

DOLMETSCH (Beechside, Haslemere, Surrey)

Dolmetsch wooden recorders, like the best American and continental makes (e.g. von Huene, Fehr, Coolsma) are expensive, and can only be obtained on order, often with several months' wait before delivery, though they can sometimes be obtained second-hand (Schott's will advise about second-hand recorders). Of impeccable craftsmanship and handsome appearance, Dolmetsch recorders combine a rich and commanding tone-quality throughout their wide compass with a broad dynamic range. The finest Dolmetsch instruments I have seen are descants and trebles. Compared with the best continental instruments they are less even in tone from one note to another, but overall less subdued and more positive in quality.

No cheap wooden descant I have seen is a better instrument than a Dolmetsch plastic one, although some quieter-toned wooden instruments are as good musically and probably more suitable for consort work. Dolmetsch plastic recorders (descant, treble and tenor with built-in thumb-rest) are excellent in intonation and produce a strong tone. The main disadvantage of plastic recorders is that they will break if dropped (accidentally) on a hard floor, and that the surface of plastic deteriorates with age with consequent breathiness of tone. Nevertheless, these plastic recorders are a better buy than most cheap wooden instruments. It is interesting that a panel of American Recorder Society examiners, asked what descants and trebles they recommended for children, favoured Dolmetsch plastic instruments (*The American Recorder*, Spring 1967, p. 53).

HEINRICH (Rudall Carte, 8–10 Denman Street, London, W.1)

Alexander Heinrich recorders are made in two main ranges. The more expensive Meister range has a narrow conical bore producing a reedy quality. The bass is end-blown and straight, the windway and fipple being under the instrument; keywork (including an interesting A flat key) makes fingering easy. In the cheaper Royal Baroque range the bass uses a crook; like the Meister bass, it favours the lower register, though not quite so fruitily. Of the remaining instruments in the Royal Baroque range, all in pearwood, the treble is much the most satisfactory, accurate, and with clear reedy high notes.

HERWIG (Rosetti, 138–140 Old Street, London, E.C.1)

Herwig was among the pioneers of recorder-making in Germany in the 1930s and succeeded in producing a large number of recorders, made of heavily wax-impregnated wood, without sacrificing quality. Herwig recorders produce a clear and solemn tone, and are probably more suited to consort playing than solo work. They are made in two qualities—'Chor', and 'Rex' (obtainable on special order only).

KÜNG (Schott & Co. Ltd., 48 Great Marlborough Street, London, W.1)

These recorders from Switzerland are made in all sizes (including great bass) and in three main qualities in a wide variety of woods including pear, rose, box, and olive. Although all three qualities are similar in design, the more expensive instruments are made of harder wood and are more highly finished; they give a clearer, more bell-like tone than the cheaper qualities. All are good, however, being easy to play and beautiful in tone, responding most warmly to lower breath-pressures; one never has to do battle with a Küng recorder to make it give of its best. They are eminently consort instruments, and are rather quiet and slow of speech for solo playing. Their lightness, true intonation, and ease of crossing the register break makes Küng instruments ideal for beginners.

MOECK (Schott's)

Moeck are probably the most enterprising of German recorder makers. The main wood used is maple, kiln-seasoned and impregnated with paraffin wax. The narrow bore design is similar to that of Küng instruments, but produces a less 'swallowed' tone-quality of great clarity and refinement. The exterior design is either plain and renaissance in style, with joints strengthened by brass rings or 'Barock' with ivory rings. Moeck instruments have a good tone range, the higher breath-pressures producing a reedier quality, though no less sweet, than low pressures.

Moeck produce a direct blown bass with a better range than most F-basses, a newly designed great bass, and a beautiful sopranino.

Moeck now make an excellent treble designed by the outstanding American maker, von Huene, and modelled on an eighteenth-century Belgian instrument by Rottenburgh. This has all the refinement of Moeck instruments, but a richer, more penetrating tone-quality, and accurate in intonation over a wide range. The Rottenburgh treble is made in three qualities—maple or plum, rosewood, and grenadilla.

MOLLENHAUER (treble only obtainable from Schott's)

The Mollenhauer treble is a lively and responsive instrument with a clear and flexible tone.

SCHOTT

Schott 'Concert' recorders are in roughly the same price range as Boosey and Hawkes and Adler 'Solo' recorders: they are obtainable in all sizes except sopranino. The treble is a strong-toned instrument, but the tenor is probably the best of the range. Intonation is generally good.

Schott plastic recorders follow the device used in Dolmetsch plastic recorders of having longitudinal striations in the floor of the windway, giving a more penetrating tone. The joint bulges are flattened at one point to stop the instrument rolling. The descant rather approaches a Dolmetsch plastic in tone, but the treble is quieter than its Dolmetsch counterpart.

The tone-quality of Schott school wooden recorders is intended to have its full effect in choral playing, and individual instruments, therefore, do not possess a commanding tone. Mr. Edgar Hunt redesigns Schott recorders periodically to achieve the best quality in mass-produced recorders at a low price.

OTHER MAKES

There are a number of makes of recorders designed mainly for school use, such as Egon Meinel (a German instrument available from Rosetti), Rosetti, Hohner, Dulcet, and some imported from the Far East. At the other extreme are fine recorders made by Stieber of Tübingen and Coolsma of

Utrecht (agent—Schott's). Coolsma recorders are elegant and even in quality, reedy and melancholy; they are individually tested by Franz Brüggen, the great Dutch recorder player. Coolsma has also made reproductions of an eighteenth-century Bressan recorder. Stieber recorders are strong and beautiful in tone, and the Stieber great bass is a particularly fine instrument, giving good intonation with ordinary fingerings through two octaves and playing up to F in the third octave; it is easy to finger and speaks quickly enough to cope with passage-work. Instruments by Robert Goble of Headington, Oxford, who stopped making recorders in the mid-50s, may still be found second-hand; they are clear, flutey and soft in tone although the intonation is not always easy to handle. Herrnsdorff 'Solist' recorders, in a medium price range, are loud and uninhibited. A number of professional players use Fehr recorders, full but restrained in sound. Klingson keyed recorders (descant, treble, tenor and bass) are made in Honduras rosewood and have six keys—tenor C, C♯, D♯, F♭¹, G♯ and B♭, which eases trill fingerings and increases the number of alternative fingerings available; they are supplied by Rudall, Carte. Rosetti supply an all-metal recorder (the Silberton). Musica Rara (2 Great Marlborough Street, London, W.1) supply a number of makes of recorder, including the German Oebra. In American music-dealers' lists one finds recorders by von Huene (magnificent), Koch and Wesner, and others called Aura, Aulos, Crown, Corelli, Concerto, Sonata, and Purcell.

SUPPLEMENT TO CHAPTER II
THE RECORDER'S REPERTOIRE

Since this book was written a great deal of music has been published for the recorder; the following is an attempt to cover significant additions to the recorder's repertoire between 1959 and 1969.

Renaissance and early seventeenth-century music

In addition to the continuation of Schott's Bibliothek series practical editions of consort music are now available in the Consortium series (Heinrichshofen, agents Hinrichsen) and in the Bläserchor series (Moeck, agents Schott). This includes much German or Netherlands music which is technically easy and, if played with verve and even percussion, can be very rewarding, for example dances by Praetorius (*Terpsichore*, 1612–Mk.), Phalèse (Louvain Dance-book 1571–H. D 2349 & Mk., and Antwerp Dance-book 1583–H. D 2350), Attaignant (Danceries 1547 and 1550–Mk.), Paul Peuerl (also U, ZfS & Ixyzet) and William Brade, an emigrant to Germany (1609–H. D 2346 and 1621–H. D 2347). Musically more demanding are the vocal and instrumental Carmina such as those in Peter Schoffer's Liederbuch (1513–N. Arch 97), the excellent collection in HM 137–8, others in N. Arch 53, S. Bib 14–16 and U/Hargail 18, and, for pieces by Ludwig Senfl, Hänssler (Novello) XI.03 and Mk., and by Isaac and Hofhaimer also Mk. The repertoire of later renaissance instrumental music, more polyphonic in nature, includes dance-settings in four and five parts by Widmann (1618–H. D 1873), Johann Staden (ZfS), and Christoph Demantius (HM 148, Consortium, ZfS & S) and in six parts by Brade (1614–H. D 2339).

Parts are now published for some of the Jacobean Consorts in Musica Britannica (S & B), nos. 3 (Ward), 4 (Lupo), 8 (Farrant and Alfonso Ferrabosco II), 9 (Thomas Simpson) and 12 (Phillips) being most suited to recorders—it is especially good to have a major six-part work of the period such as Peter Phillip's Passamezzo Pavan (no. 12) so readily available: there is more Ferrabosco in S. Bib and Consortium. Consorts are also available reprinted from *Music of Scotland* and *Music at the Court of King Henry VIII* in the same series (S & B).

The solo descant or tenor player may take his pleasure in *Der Fluiten Lust-Hof* (1646) of Jacob van Eyck, published complete in three volumes (S: brief selections in U and S). Some excellent two-part music was composed in this period, including the Rhaw collection (1545–H. D 2338), fugues by Demantius (H. D 2342), and pieces from Schultz' *Musikalischer Lustgarten* (1622–H. D 1362

& ZfS—more Schultz (in four and eight parts) also in Consortium).

Three-part consorts by John Jenkins (HM 149; see also U) are
also among recent publications, though they require some
'arranging', especially in the bass line. Editions of dances by
Frescobaldi (Mitteldeutscher) and canzonets by Monteverdi (U)
provide more music of great interest for recorder trio, together with
John Hilton's Fantazias in H. D 2348 with their alternating directions of 'softly' and 'away'.

The repertoire of four-part consort music is enhanced by Fantasias by Banchieri (S. Ant. and ZfS), Vecchi, Scheidt and Ravenscroft (S. Bib), and a delightful Canzona a la Francese by Jan de
Macque (S. Bib). Short four-part Ricercari by the lutenist Vin-
cenzo Galilei, father of the astronomer, are published by Schott,
and some of his madrigals and canzonette in H. D 2149. More
Holborne in five parts is available (S. Bib), together with a series
of Lachrimae settings by Holborne, Brade and Phillips (H. D
2175). Pieces by Tomkins are available in U and Consortium.
Although little of the fine consort music by William Lawes in
Musica Britannica suits a consort of recorders alone (because of
the range of the bass part), some Lawes is available in U and
Consortium (H. D 2340). Thomas Simpson's Taffel Consort
(1621–H. D 1794) contains some rewarding pieces for quartet and
general bass, especially the opening Ballet by Simpson himself.

Larger consorts will revel in Tiburtio Massaino's eight-part
Canzona (U), and seven- (H. D 2172), eight- (H. D 1585 & 2078)
and twelve-part (H. D 2173 & U-Canzona XIII) pieces by
Gabrieli, Frescobaldi and others, and, at the end of the period,
Dietrich Becker's Suite for five recorders and keyboard (U) and
Purcell's great six- and seven-part In Nomines (Faber).

Baroque and eighteenth-century period

The record player's Purcell repertoire now includes publications
of the duet 'Hark, how the Songsters' from the masque in *Timon
of Athens* (S), the chamber cantata 'How pleasant is this flowery
plain and grove' (HM 164) and some quartet arrangements from
Abdelazar (S). An article by Walter Bergmann on Purcell's use of
the recorder, with a complete list of his compositions for the instrument, appeared in the November 1965 issue of *The Recorder and
Music Magazine*. In the Purcellian manner is a duet by Philip
Hart, 'Proceed, sweet charmer of the ear' for two soprano voices,
two trebles and keyboard (S), and four little suites for treble and
keyboard by George Bingham (S). The Daniel Purcell repertoire
is enlarged by three trio-sonatas (two in S, one Faber). Arias by
Handel, including 'Angeletti che cantare' from *Rinaldo* (referred

to on p. 19), are published by Sikorski. The pastoral scene (and the sopranino repertoire) is further enriched by two Arne pieces (both S), 'The Morning' and 'A Wood Nymph', the latter dated as late as 1771, and by Galliard's 'How Sweet the Warbling Linnet Sings' from *Pan and Syrinx* (U). More of the J. B. Loeillets' (London and Ghent) solo and trio-sonatas are published in HM 162 & 165 (these solo sonatas are not duplicated in the Mk. editions from op. 1 and the S editions from op. 3), in U/BMI (12 sonatas op. 2), in HM 166, 176 and 181 (trio-sonatas with oboe) and Mk. More of Schickhard's music is available in the form of solo sonatas (S, and the excellent op. 7 sonatas, especially no. 7, in Mk.), a trio-sonata (S) and three sonorous sonatas for treble, two oboes and continuo (H/Lienau). Six imaginative Barsanti sonatas are available, three with good continuo realisations in S, and three less well done in HM 183–5. Among other contributions from musical immigrants to England are two sets of Ayrs for treble, violin and continuo by Matteis (S), Divertimenti by Bononcini (S), six suites for two trebles and keyboard (S) and some good duets without keyboard (S) by Paisible, and a good sonata from a set of six (S) and some suites (Mk.) by Dieupart for treble and keyboard; the latter are transcribed for recorder on Dieupart's instructions from his superb harpsichord suites, two of which were copied by hand by J. S. Bach. Pepusch's work is made better known by a pleasing double trio-sonata (2 Tr, 2 V & Bc) (S), two further solo sonatas (S), a cantata for soprano voice, treble and continuo (Faber), and a trio-sonata with viola (HM 161), Sammartini's by an exciting concerto for descant recorder and strings (S) and a galant solo sonata (H/Noetzel), and Finger's by an elegant trio-sonata with oboe (Na MP 26) and two sonatas for three trebles (S). Thurston Dart has edited three unusual works (all OUP) a trio-sonata by Nicolas Derosier commemorating 'La Fuite du Roy d'Angleterre' (James II) in 1688, a trio-sonata in imitation of birds by William Williams and a sonata by Andrew Parcham with a curiously rhapsodic last movement. He also argues that Handel's Op. 3 no. 3 Concerto Grosso was scored for the bird flageolet in G, and OUP publishes the work for descant recorder and strings. Three of Woodcock's concertos, two for one descant and strings (U. Hargail, and Chester/Hanson or Faber) and the other for two descants and strings (S), together with a further Baston concerto (Hänssler), increase the recorder's repertoire of champagne-style sixth-flute music.

Publishing over the last ten years has made available playing editions of some of the best works which include recorders. Apart from Blow's Ode on the Death of Mr. Henry Purcell (S), and Corelli's 'La Follia' variations (H. D 1314 and U), many vocal and instrumental works with recorders by Schütz, J. S. Bach and Telemann are included in the Hänssler and Bärenreiter catalogues. Some Telemann pieces with other wind instruments are available, such as a trio-sonata in F with horn (H. D 1843), a concerto for recorder and bassoon (H/Heinrichshofen), a magnificent concerto for two trebles, two oboes, two violins and continuo (S), an overture for two trebles, two oboes and strings (U/Harmonia or Novello/Möseler–Corona 97) and an excellent trio-sonata in A minor for treble, oboe and continuo (S or Hänssler) (two further trio-sonatas for the same group in HM 194 & 195). Telemann's A minor concerto for recorder, viola de gamba, strings and continuo, one of the few works in the recorder's repertoire which can be accounted great music, is published by Mk., together with a C major concerto for recorder alone. Moeck also publish a concerto by Graun for recorder, violin and strings, and a concerto a 6 for two trebles, two oboes and two bassoons by Pierre Prowo. Equally worthy of revival in the field of German music are sonatas for three trebles by Scherer (S), trio-sonatas by Prowo (Mk) and four tuneful suites by J. C. Schultze (Mk. S).

More of Vivaldi's recorder music is at last available in practical editions. Musica Rara publish a fine and difficult trio-sonata with bassoon, two (much easier) concerti in D major for treble, oboe, violin, bassoon and continuo (P. 204–La Pastorella, and P. 201, almost a violin concerto), and a bold concerto in C (P. 81) for treble, oboe, two violins and continuo. Schott and Eulenberg (also S) publish a fine virtuoso sopranino concerto in C, and, as elegant but without the fireworks, a concerto in A minor for recorder, two violins and continuo. All twelve of Veracini's sonatas of 1716 are published by H/Peters (or some also in U or Ba). Sonatas by Martino Bitti are published in HM 190–1, as simple though less effective than Marcello's sonatas (HM 142, 151–2, S and U/Hargail, Mk.—tr and Kd; Sikorski—2 trs). Two Sinfonie by Alessandro Scarlatti for treble and keyboard are published by Suddeutscher (H), and the superb Sinfonia XII in C minor for treble and strings in HM 168. S publish a rewarding solo sonata by Diogenio Bigaglia. Two Corelli and a Schickhard trio-sonata are arranged with guitar continuo, together with some solo sonatas by Handel, Loeillet and Pepusch, in U/Doblinger.

The elusive French style can be studied in Faber's publication of Preludes by Freillon-Poncein and Hotteterre le Romain, especially in conjunction with David Lasocki's edited translation (Barrie and Rockcliff) of Hotteterre's *Principes* (see also Hotteterre—Duo and Rondeau (S)). Faber also publish Hotteterre's Suite in F. These principles may then be applied to Delavigne's attractive Suite 'Les Fleurs' for treble and tenor (Ixyzet) and the six suites edited by

Vellekoop (Ixyzet). Six Delavigne sonatas are published by H/Heinrichshofen, S publish a trio-sonata in D and some very easy duets by Boismortier, and U/BMI a duet by Monteclair. Some attractive recorder music by Naudot has recently been published, being two excellent concertos for treble, two violins and continuo in HM 153 and S, two trios (S), a sonata (HM 182) and some simple duets called 'Babioles' (S). Two of the elder Chédeville's Sonatilles Galantes are published in H. D 1294 and 1301. The culminating challenges of French music are Couperin's Concerts Royaux for two treble instruments (e.g. tenor and violin) and continuo and (but only partly suitable) Rameau's Pièces de Clavecin en Concerts (United Music Publishers/Durand).

Eighteenth-century arrangements

An unexpectedly successful piece of piracy is the Ricordi edition of eight pieces from Bach's unaccompanied suites for 'cello. Bach fugues are predictably rewarding in arrangement (by Duschesnes in U/BMI, Contrapuncti I and III from *The Art of Fugue* in U/Hargail); some earlier fugues for quartet are in H. D 2198 and D. 2318, and U (Pachelbel). Further excursions in Vivaldi (MR P 82 & P 360) and Telemann (H. D 2063 & D. 2360) need little justification, and two quartets by Carl Stamitz for treble, two violins and 'cello (S. Ant.) provide a gratifying addition to the recorder's repertoire, as do sonatas by Bréval and Leclair (H/Noetzel). Mozart's Andante in F (K. 315) for flute and strings (S) suits the treble recorder so well that one is even tempted to imagine Mozart had that instrument in mind. On an altogether different plane, the eight short duets (for two flutes) by Geuss (Mk.)—especially no. 7—provide two tenor players with some pleasant frivolity.

Modern Music

The interest shown by modern composers in the recorder as shown by publication over the last ten years is extremely gratifying. A number of major British composers have produced important additions to the recorder's repertoire. Edmund Rubbra has written a short quartet 'Notturno', a Passacaglia Sopra 'Plusieurs Regrets' for treble and keyboard, and a full-length sonatina (all Lengnick) first performed, like much other new music for recorders, at Carl Dolmetsch's annual Wigmore Hall concert. Rubbra's work is rhapsodic, and replete with enharmonic changes; and the last movement of the sonatina, typically, is based on a sixteenth-century Spanish tune. Arnold Cooke's music (Suite for treble and keyboard—S, Suite for recorder quartet—Zfs) is vigorous and impressive, Wilfred Mellers' (Sonatina—S, Eclogue

for treble, violin, 'cello, harpsichord and optional percussion—
Novello) more remote but intellectually rewarding. Lennox
Berkeley's Concertino for treble, violin, 'cello and harpsichord
(Chester) has the same clarity of form and melodic and harmonic
energy as his Sonatina. Most of this music is technically difficult;
less demanding are Gordon Jacob's Variations (MR) and Sonata
(MR) for treble and keyboard, and Hans Gal's Concertino (U),
all interesting and competent compositions. John Graves has
written a gay Divertimento for treble and piano; and John
Gardner a little Suite for treble and piano (OUP), which is a more
significant work than its name suggests, and an as yet unpublished
Concerto (Wigmore Hall, 1968). Colin Hand (OUP) and Ronald
Finch (S) have written good though not profound sonatas for
treble and piano. The descant soloist is served, among various
frivolities, by a pleasing suite by Christopher Steel (Novello), and
by a major work, Walter Bergmann's Sonata (S).

Although no composer has equalled Michael Tippett's inspira-
tion in writing for two recorders (Four Inventions—S), the reper-
toire of modern music for two recorders has been improved by good
duets for treble and tenor by Francis Chagrin (S) and Michael
Maxwell (S). Worthy of mention are Georges Migot's fluent
Suite (Ba), Eric Roseberry's Three Aphorisms (U), and duets by
Arthur Butterworth and Serge Lancen in Hinrichsen's 'Equal
Pitch' series. Among recorder trios the best recent compositions
include James Butt's 'September Diary' (Galliard), Jeannine
Vanier's Fantasia (U/BMI), Thomas Northwood's Fantasia on a
Minuet and Anthony Milner's 'Corfu' (U). York Bowen has
written two pleasant pieces for recorder trio with keyboard (U),
and Dulcie Holland a Sonatina for two descants and piano
(U/BMI). Francis Baines' fiery quartet (S) produces sounds
which, for all their originality, are alien to recorders.

Publications of modern German recorder music are dominated
by the compositions of two recorder virtuosi, Hans-Martin Linde
and Hans Ulrich Staeps, both of whom write interesting and varied
music in an idiom which suits the recorder perfectly; Linde's style
is fluent, Staeps's more forceful. They both use a wide range of
instrumentation. Linde's Serenata à Tre (S) uses descant, treble
and bass in turn as the solo instrument with 'cello and guitar, and
he has also written a trio for recorder, flute and keyboard (S).
Both Linde and Staeps have written well for solo treble (e.g.
Staeps—Virtuoso Suite (S), Linde—Inventions (H. D 1369) and
Divertimento with percussion (ZfS)). Linde has written a most
interesting Sonatine Française for descant and piano (Hänssler/
Novello), and a trio for treble/sopranino, tenor and bass (Hänssler).
A good example of Staeps's musical energy is his Partita on 'Est-ce

Mars' for recorder quartet (ZfS). Staeps's music is often at its best when it is simple, as for example in the Chorisches Quintett (U), but there are very good things in most of his pieces. The difference in quality between Staeps and his contemporaries is illustrated by the lack of effectiveness of the same idiom in Dietfried Barnet's Caprices (U). Other German recorder composers still write in the Hausmusik style, though Eric Leber's trio (H. D 2328) is quite piquant. On the other hand there are some German composers who are breaking new ground, not simply by using very high notes as in Konrad Lechner's 'Metamorphosen' for treble and keyboard (Hänssler), but by tonguing and fingering techniques as in Jurg Baur's three interesting works Incontri (1960) for treble and piano, Mutazioni (1962) for treble solo, inspired by the mosaic forms of the Cosmati in Rome, and, slightly less profound in conception, Pezzi Ucelli (1964) for treble solo (all published by Breitkopf). Even more avant-garde is Luciano Berio's 'Gesti' (U) with a pattern of fingering independent of sounds made by the mouth and voice.

Modern composers have experimented with new combinations of recorders with other instruments. Martinu's 'Pastorals' (Ba), an important work for recorders, uses a choir of two descants, two tenors and bass with clarinet, two violins and 'cello; Townsend's 'Variations on a Theme of Milhaud' (H) uses descant recorder with B♭ trumpet, 'cello and piano and Helmut Eder's 'Divertimentino' (Heinrichshofen) uses treble with C trumpet, fiddle and bass; Beyer's 'Tiento' (Ba) is for recorder and organ; and Krenek's 'Quintina über die fünf Vokale' is for treble recorder, vibraphone, xylophone, guitar, viola and percussion. May experimentation continue!

TABLE OF NORMAL FINGERINGS ON THE TREBLE RECORDER

(for alternative fingerings see Chapter VIII)

LOWER OCTAVE

	F	F#/Gb	G	G#/Ab	A	A#/Bb	B	C	C#/Db	D	D#/Eb	E	F'
0	●	●	●	●	●	●	●	●	●	●	●	●	●
1	●	●	●	●	●	●	●	●	●	●	●	●	○
2	●	●	●	●	●	●	●	●	●	●	○	○	●
3	●	●	●	●	●	●	●	●	○	○	●	○	○
4	●	●	●	●	●	●	○	○	●	○	●	○	○
5	●	●	●	●	●	○	●	○	●	○	○	○	○
6	●●	●●	●●	●○	○○	●●	●●	○○	○○	○○	○○	○○	○○
7	●●	●○	○○	○○	○○	●●	○○	○○	○○	○○	○○	○○	○○

UPPER OCTAVE

(for thumbing apertures and further high notes see Chapter IX)

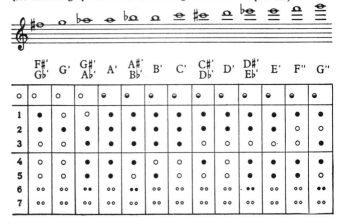

	F#'/Gb'	G'	G#'/Ab'	A'	A#'/Bb'	B'	C'	C#'/Db'	D'	D#'/Eb'	E'	F''	G''
0	○	○	○	◑	◑	◑	◑	◑	◑	◑	◑	◑	◑
1	●	○	○	●	●	●	●	●	●	●	●	●	●
2	●	●	●	●	●	●	●	●	●	●	○	○	○
3	○	○	●	●	●	●	●	○	○	○	○	○	●
4	○	○	●	●	●	○	○	●	○	●	●	●	●
5	○	○	●	●	○	●	○	○	○	●	●	●	○
6	○○	○○	●●	○○	●●	○○	○○	○○	○○	●●	○○	○○	●●
7	○○	○○	○○	○○	○○	○○	○○	○○	○○	○○	○○	○○	○○

INDEX

Abdelazar (Purcell) 142
Abel 25
Acciaccatura **118**
Acis and Galatea (Handel) 19
Addison 19
Adler r's 38, **136–7**
Adson 15
Agricola 3, 11
Ahle 19
Albion and Albanius (Dryden-Grabu) 4
Alpine Suite (Britten) 27, 110
Alternative fingerings 40, 70–1, **74–90, 93–6** (high notes), 99, **109–10** (tone), **118–20** (trills), 125, 133
Alto clef 14, 126, **127**
'Alto' r. 36
American Recorder Society 137
Amplification of r. tone 98
And So to Bed (Ellis) 28
Antiquity of r. 1
Appoggiatura 76, 84, 85, **115,** 116, 117, 118, 120
Apted Book 26
Arbeau 25
Archive series (Schott) 10 etc., **15**
Arne 19, 25, 143
Arnold, Malcolm 27
Arrangements 22, 23, 24, **25–6,** 65, 145
Art of Fugue, The (Bach) 23, 145
Arts Theatre Club 28
Attack (see also Tonguing) **61–2, 101,** 109
Attaignant 13, 141
Aubert 22
Au Clair de la Lune 45, 46
Augener (publishers) 25, 26, 56

Babell 19
Bach, C. P. E. 24, 113, 121
Bach, J. C. 24, 25
Bach, J. S. 4, 17, **19–20,** 23–4, 36, 79, 116, 121, 123, 127, 143, 144, 145

Bach, W. F. 24
Back to Methuselah (Shaw) 28
Bacon, Francis 17, 28, 30, 33, 105
Baines, Anthony 98, 107
Baines, Francis 27, 146
Bakelite (see also 'Plastic') 33
Bamboo pipes 27
Banchieri 142
Bannister 5
Barbier de Seville, Le (Paisiello) 23
Bärenreiter (publishers) 10 etc., 141 etc.
Barnet, Dietfried 147
Baroque music **16–23,** 26, **142–5**
Baroque r. 32–3
Barre, Michel de la 21, 22
Barrie and Rockliff (publishers) 144
Barsanti 18, 143
Baryton trios (Haydn) 24
Bassano 12
Bass clef 38, 126
Bass r. 3, 11, 12, 17, 24, 26, **38, 54, 97** (fingering), 98, 126, 135, 137, 138, 139
Bassoon 22, 23, 38, 144
Baston 19, 143
Bate, Stanley 27
Baur, Jurg 147
Beats **72–3**
Beaujoyeaux 16
Becker 142
Bergmann, Walter 17, 24, 26, 42, 48, 142, 146
Berio, Luciano 147
Berkeley, Lennox 27, 65, 125, 146
Bertali 21
Beyer 147
Biber 21
Bibliothek series (Schott) 141
Bicinia 11, 14
Bigaglia 144
Bilney 4
Binding a joint 35
Bingham 142

Bird Fancyer's Delight, The (ed. Godman) 2
Bitti 144
Blavet 25
Blockflöte 30
Blow 4, 18, 143
'Blowing out' 105
BMI (Canada) (publishers) 143, 145, 146
Boalch 15
Boccherini 25
Boehm 7
Boismortier 22, 145
Book of Martyrs (Foxe) 4
Bononcini 18, 143
Boosey and Hawkes (music and instruments) 10 etc., 65, 137
Bore 1, 29, 31, **32–3,** 34, 37, 98, **104–5** (tone), 110, 134, 136, 138
Bowen, York 146
Boyce 25
Box-wood 33, 34, 138
Brade 141, 142
Brandenburg Concertos (Bach) 24, 36, 123
Brass 33, 139
'Break'—see Overblowing
Breathing 38, 45, **53–8,** 123, 132
Breath-marks 54, **130–2**
Breath-pressure 1, 29–30, 37, 44, 45, 46, 48, 49, **53–8,** 60, 65, **66–7** (intonation), 69, 78, 80, 88, 92, **98–100** (volume), 102, 103, **106** (tone), 110, 114, 119, 123, 124, 126
Breitkopf and Härtel (publishers) 10 etc., 147
Breslau, Anonymous Master of 21
Bréval 145
British Standard (pitch and 'kite-mark') 136
Britten, Benjamin 27, 28, 65, 110
Broken consort 12, 16
Browning (Byrd) 14–15
Brüggen, Franz 140
Bull 15
Burghardt, Hans Georg 28
Burrows, Benjamin 28

Bushing of thumb-hole 35, 92–3, 104
Butt, James 146
Butterworth, Arthur 146
Buttress-finger technique **90**
Buxtehude 26
Byrd 12, 14, 52

Cadential trill 113, 115, **116–17,** 118, **120**
Caix d'Hervelois, de 21, 22
Cantatas 19–20, 21, 22, 26, 28
Canzona 13, 14
Canzonets (Morley) 15
Capriol Suite (Warlock) 26
Care of r. **34–6**
Carmina 141
Carols 11
Carr 5, 6
Castle, Zillah 28
Cello 20, 24, 38, 145, 146, 147
Chaconne 17, 26, 130, 133
Chagrin, Francis 146
Chaucer 2, 10
Chédeville 22, 143
Chester (publishers) 143, 146
Choosing an instrument **39–40,** 136–140
Choral prelude 14, 23–4
Chromatic runs 65, 76, 125
Chopin 13
Cittern 16, 17
Clarinet 1, 110, 122, 147
Cleaning the r. **36,** 104–5
Clefs 7, 14, 38, **126–7**
'Clicks' **47,** 51, 56, **62–3,** 74, **76,** 86, 87, 94, 96, 110, 122, 137
Clogging of windway 105, 135
Commonwealth 5
Condensation 33, 34, 93, 102, **105–6,** 135, 137, 139
Consortium series 141, 142
Consort Lessons (Morley) 17
Consort Player, The 15, 16
Consort playing, 11–16, 21, 23–4, 26, 27, 28, 32, 37, 38, 39, 41, 51, 55, 57, 66, 69, 107, 109, 110, 114, 126, 130–1, **131–2,** 133, 134, 135, 137, 139
Contrabass 3

Cooke, Arnold 27, 145
Coolsma r's 137
Coperario 16
Corelli 18, 112, 143, 144
Cork joints 31, 35
Corner of room, reflection of sound from 45, 56, 135
Cornett 13, 14, 15, 16
'Corona' series 10 etc., **14,** 144
Corteccia 16
Couperin 22, 113, 120, 145
Cracks in r. 35, 36, 40
Cramer (publishers) 27
Crescendo 40, 100, 134
Croft 18, 19
Croker, Norris 56
Cross-fingering **48,** 49, 59, 91, 109
Curwen (publishers) 16

Dallas 136
Dance music 10, 11, 14, 25–6, 48, 127, 129, 141
Dannreuther, Edward 120
Dart, Thurston 120, 143
Decrescendo 56, **77,** 80, 100, 132
Deering 15
Demantius 141
Derivation of word 'recorder' 2
Derosier 143
Descant r. 2, 19, 24, **37,** 41, 42, 57, 90, 91, 98, 110, 126, 135, **136–40** (makes), 141, 143, 146, 147
Description of r. **29–39**
Deutscher Ricordi Verlag 10 etc.
Dewey, Monica 48
Diaphragm 53–4, 108
Dieupart 143
Difference tones **72–3,** 109
Diminuendo 100
Dinn, Freda 26, 41
Dioclesian (Purcell) 17
Divisions 18, 120, 133
Doblinger (publishers) 144
Dolmetsch, Arnold 8, 120
Dolmetsch, Carl F. 8, 27, 42, 95, 102, 110, 113, 145
Dolmetsch, Mabel 8, 129
Dolmetsch r's 136, **137,** 139
Donington, Robert 121
Dotted notes **64,** 115, 117, 129

Double-forked fingerings **74,** 80, 84
Double tonguing **63–4,** 65, 109, 120, 129
Doucet 2
Dowland 12, 14, 52
Dryden 4
Dufay 11
Dulcet r's 139
Dunstable 11
Duschesnes 145
Dynamics (see also Volume) **132–3**

Earliest illustrations of r. 1–2, 32
Earliest r's 2
Earliest references to r. 2
Earliest use of r. 10–11, 16–17
East 15
Easter Oratorio (Bach) 20
Ebonite 139
Ebony wood 33
Echo effects 63, 67, **101–2,** 133
Echo key **103,** 110
Echo tonguing **63,** 103
Eder Helmut 147
Edge 29–32, 34, 59, 104, 105
Edge-tone **29**
Eighteenth-century music **23–7,** 64, 133, 142–5
Elbows, 42, 43, 46
Elizabethan music 3, 11, 15, 32, 141–2
Elizabeth, Queen 3
Ellis, Vivian 28
Emery, Walter 121
Ending a note **65**
English Chamber Music (Meyer) 13
English music 13, **14–19, 27–8,** 132, 142–3, 145–6
Essay on the True Art of Playing Keyboard Instruments (C. P. E. Bach) 121
Essercizii Musici (Telemann) 20
Esther (Handel) 25
Etymology of word 'recorder' **2**
Eulenberg (publishers) 144
Evelyn 18
Exercises, physical, for fingers 124
Extemporization 120
Eyck, Jacob van 141

Faber (publishers) 142, 143, 144
Farnaby 12, 15
Farrant 141
Fasch 21
Fatigue of fingers 124
Fehr r's 137, 140
Fellowes, E. H. 14
Ferrabosco 16, 141
Fesch, de 25
Fifteen Solos 63
Figured bass 115
Finch, Ronald 146
Finger, Godfrey 18, 143
Fingering 6–7, 8, 37, 41, **42–51**
    (normal), 62, **67–71** (intona-
    tion), **74–91** (alternatives), **93–7**
    (high notes), **99–100** (volume),
    109 (tone), **118–120** (orna-
    mentation), **124–5**, 126, 127,
    133–4, 135, 147, **148** (chart)
Finger-pad 42–4, 49
Filtz 25
Fipple 1, **30**
Flageolet 1, 29, 30, 143
Flattening—see Intonation
Flautino alla vigesima seconda
    16
Flauto piccolo 19
Flourish 114, **117–18,** 120
Flute 1, **6–7,** 16, 17, 20, 21, 22, 23,
    24, 25, 29, 30, 31, 90, 104, 107,
    122, 127, 145, 146
Flûte à bec 6, 21, 30
Flûte à neuf trous 3, 42
Flute-clock 24
Flûte d'Angleterre 3, 6
Flûte douce 3, 6, 18, 98, 111
Flutter tonguing 65
Follia 18, 143
Fontegara (Ganassi) 3, 42, 60, 121,
Foot section of r. **30–1,** 32, 35, 49,
    134
Forked   fingerings,   59–60,   69,
    70–1, 74–5, 81, 84, 88, 90,
    99–100, 119
Form of music 130–1
Foxe 4
Franck, Melchior 14
Frederick the Great 21
Freillon-Poncein 144

French music 5, 6, 11, **13–14,** 17,
    21–2, 23, 113, 120, 144–5
French violin clef 7, 126
Frescobaldi 26, 142
Fricker, Racine 27
Fugue 14, 28
Funccius 21

Gabrieli 12, 13, 142
Gadgets **71,** 102, 110
Gal, Hans 146
Galilei 142
Galliard 18, 143
Galliard (publishers) 146
Galpin, Canon F. W. 1
Ganassi 3, 42, 60, 121
Gardner, John 146
Gascoigne 3
Gastoldi 13
German fingering, 8, 48, **91**
German flute 6, 7
German music 8, 13, **14, 19–21,**
    24, 25, **28,** 141, 143–4, 146–7
Gervaise 13
Genzmer, Harald 28
Geuss 145
Ghiselin 11
Gibbons, Orlando 15
Giesbert, F. J. 42, 90
Glanville-Hicks, Peggy 96
Gluck 23
Goble r's 140
Godman, Stanley 2, 61
Gorboduc (Norton and Sackville) 3
Grace note 118
Graun 144
Graupner 21
Graves, John 146
Great bass r. 3, **38–9,** 97, 136, 139,
    140
Grenadilla 139
'Grope, press, pat and hammer'
    method of fingering **43–4,** 46,
    49, 51
Ground bass, 17, 18, 131
Grove's Dictionary 121
Guitar 28, 144, 146, 147

Half-holes 29, 42, 46, 49, **50–1,** 68,
    69, 71, 78, 120

Hamlet 3, 32, 37, 41, 59
Hammer-blow method of fingering **43,** 44, 45, 46, 49, 51, 119, 120, 124
Hand, Colin 146
Handbook for Singers (Croker) 56
Handel 6, 18, **19,** 22, 25, 27, 36, 37, 112, 127, 142, 143, 144
Hands, position of 31, **42–3,** 46, 47, 51, 119–20
Hänssler (publishers) 141, 143, 144, 146, 147
Hare and Walsh 5
Hargail (publishers) 141 etc.
Harmonics 29, 30, 39, 44, 109
Harp 16
Harpsichord 16, 20, 63, 103, 143, 146
Hart 142
Haslemere Festival 8, 112
Haslinger edition 28
Hassler 14
Haydn 24
Heat treatment of woods 33
Heinichen 21
Heinrich r's 138
Heinrichshofen (publishers) 141, 144, 145, 147
Henry VII 3
Henry VIII 3, 141
Herrnsdorf r's 140
Herwig 138
Herwiga r's 137–8
High notes 29, 32, 35, 39, 61, 90, **92–7,** 108, 123–4, 147
Hilton 16, 142
Hindemith 28
Hinrichsen (publishers) 10 etc., 61, 141 etc.
History of the r. **1–9**
Hofhaimer 141
Holborne 5, 15, 142
Holinshed 3
Holland, Dulcie 146
Hook, James 24, 48
Hortus Musicus series 10 etc., 141 etc.
Hopkins, Antony 27, 28
Horn 144

Hotteterre-le-Romain 5, 57, 60, 90, 113, 144
Hudgebut 5
Hume 16
Hunt, Edgar 8, 42, 139
Hymn tunes 45, 55, 58

Illustrations of r. **1–2,** 32
Impregnation of woods 33, 34, 136, 138
Improvisation 112, 131, 133
'In-between' notes 47, 56, 74
In Dulci Jubilo 14, 26
In Nomine 15, 16, 128, 142
Interpretation of Music, The (Dart) 120
Interpretation of the Music of the 17th and 18th Centuries, The (Dolmetsch) 120
Intonation 38, 39, 54, **66–73,** 77, 78–90, 93–6, 99, 103, 123, 134
Isaac 11, 141
Italian music 4, 12, **13,** 14, 16–17, **22–3,** 26, 113, 132, 144
Ives 16
Ivory 3, 31, 33, 35, 93, 139
Ixyzet (publishers) 141, 144, 145

Jacob, Gordon 27, 146
Jacobean music 3, 15–16, 141, 142
Jacobs, Manuel 27
Jenkins 16, 142
Jentsch, Walter 28
Jocasta (Gascoigne) 3, 4
Joints 31, **35,** 40, 105
Jonson 2
Josquin des Près 11
Jumps over intervals 63, 83, 86, 87, 88, **125**

Kenilworth 3
Key mechanism **6–7,** 37, **38,** 90, 95, 103, 104, 110, 140
Kiln treatment of woods 33, 138
King Arthur (Purcell) 18
Kleine Kammermusik (Telemann) 21
Knab, Armin 28
Knee 78
'Knick'-system (Adler) bass r's 38, 137

Koerppen, Alfred 28
Krenek 147
Küng r's 136, 138

Lachrimae (Dowland) 14, 142
Lancen, Serge 146
Lanolin 35
Lasocki, David 144
Lassus 14
Lawes, William 16, 142
Leading **134**
'Leaking' fingering **95–7**
Leber, Eric 147
Lechner, Konrad 147
Leclair 145
Lefkovitch, Leonard 113
Legato 51, **62,** 63
Leigh, Walter 27
Lengnick (publishers) 27, 145
Length of notes 61, 62, 101
Lerich, Rudolf 28
Lessons for Consort (Rosseter) 17
Liber Fridolini Sichery 11
Lienau (publishers) 143
'Lift' 129
Linde, Hans-Martin 146–7
Little finger of the left hand 43, 69,
    79, 134
Little-finger shading **69,** 89
Lips 29, 30, **44,** 53, 54, 65, 100, 107
Lloyd, Ll. S. 29
Locke 16, 26
Locke Nur (Telemann) 21
Loeillet 18, 21, 143, 144
London Trios (Haydn) 24
Longman and Broderip 6
Long notes 45, 54, 123, 132
Loose joints 35
Lorelei r's 138
Lost Tradition in Music, The
    (Rothschild) 130
Low trilling **79,** 88
Lully 17
Lungs 45, 53, 54, 132, 134
Lupo 16, 141
Lute 12, 15, 16, 17

Machaut 27
Macque, Jan de 142
Magnificat (Bach) 20

Makes of r's 40, **136–40**
Making Music 41
Manifold, J. S. 4
Maple 33, 138, 139
Marais, Marin 21, 22
Marcello 23, 144
Marston 3
Martinu 147
Massage 124
Massaino 142
Massinger 4
Materials used in making r. 30, 31,
    33–4, 98, 136–40
Matteis 143
Mattheson 21
Maxwell, Michael 146
Medieval music **10–11,** 57
Meech, Michael 26
Mellers, Wilfred 145–6
Mersenne 3
Method for the r. in F (Giesbert) 42,
    90
Metronome 119, 126, 130, 133
Meyer, Ernst 13
Mico 15
Migot, Georges 146
Mikado, The (Sullivan) 26
Milford, Robin 27, 28
Milner, Anthony 146
Milner, Arthur 27
Milton 4
Milton (Senior) 5
Mitchell, W. J. 121
Mitteldeutscher Verlag 23, 142
Modern music **27–8,** 108, 117,
    145–7
Moeck (music and instruments)
    10 etc., 136, 138–9, 141 etc.
Mollenhauer r's 139
Monteclair 145
Monteverdi 16–17, 142
Moore, Timothy 27
Mops, r. 34
Mordent 86, 89, 112, 113, **114–15,**
    120
Morley 15, 17, 52
Möseler (publishers) 10 etc.
Mouth 44, 53–4
Mozart 7, 23, 24, 145
Müller-Hartmann, R. 28

Mulliner Book, The 15
Murrill, Herbert 27, 108, 117
Musica Britannica, 11, 12, 15, 141, 142
Musica getutscht (Virdung) 2, 32
Musical Offering (Bach) 23
Musical Ornamentation (Dannreuther) 120
Music and Letters 8
Music and Sound (Lloyd) 29
Musica Rara (publishers) 10 etc., 140, 144, 146
Music in English Drama, The (Manifold) 4
Music in the Renaissance (Reese) 12
Music Press edition 113
Muting **102**

Nagel (publishers) 10 etc.
National Portrait Gallery 17
Natural History (Bacon) 17, 28, 33, 106
Naudot 22, 145
Nel Dolce dell' oblio (Handel) 19
Newman, Joel 19
Noble, Robert 41
Noetzel (publishers) 143, 145
Northwood, Thomas 146
Norton and Sackville 3
Novello (publishers) 10 etc., 141 etc.
Noyes Fludde (Britten) 28, 65

Oboe 1, 8, 9, 19, 20, 22, 23, 25, 54, 123, 143, 144
Oblique cutting of holes 37, 47
Obrecht 11
Octaving (see also Thumbing) 1, **49**
Ode on St. Cecilia's Day (Purcell) 17
Ode on the Birthday of Queen Mary (Purcell) 18
Ode on the Death of Mr. Henry Purcell (Blow) 18, 143
Oiling the r. 34–5
Okeghem 11
Old English Instruments of Music (Galpin) 1–2
Olive oil 34, 124
Olive-wood 33, 138
Orchésographie (Arbeau) 25

Orfeo (Gluck) 23
Orfeo (Monteverdi) 16–17
Organ 4, 12, 24, 26, 72, 147
Ornamentation (see also under individual ornaments, e.g. Trill) **112–121, 133**
Overblowing (the breath-pressure 'break') 1, 30, 50, **55,** 59, 88, 89, 93, 101, 103, 107, 114, 119
Overture in the French style 64, 129
Oxford Books of R. Pieces 42
Oxford Orchestral Series 25
Oxford University Press 10 etc., 42, 117, 141 etc.

Pachelbel 145
Padovano 12
Paisible 18, 143
Paisiello 23
Palestrina 12, 13, 52
Palisander wood 33
Palsgrave 3
Pan and Syrinx (Galliard) 143
Paradise Lost 4
Paraffin wax 33, 138
Parcham 143
Parthenia 15
Passage work 63, 74, **77**, 82, 88, 101, 123, 125, 132
Passing trill 116
Pastor Fido, Il (Vivaldi) 23
Pastoral associations of r. 4, 19, 143
Paterson (publishers) 27
Pause before articulation 115, 116, 120
Pearwood 33, 38, 138
Pepusch 18, 19, 143, 144
Pepys 4, 6, 28
Performance 74, 81, 99, 123, **128–135**
Peter, Hildemarie 33, **61,** 118
Penerl 141
Phalèse 141
Philibert de la Vigne 22
Phillips 141, 142
Phrasing 32, 38, 47, 56, 78, 85, 87, 99–101, 106, 108, 113, 129, **130–2,** 134

Piano 29, 38, 67, 76, 108, 134, 135
'Pinching' (see Thumbing) **50,** 69, **83,** 93
Pivot thumbing **83–4,** 87, 88
Plaine & Easy Introduction to Practicall Musicke, A (Morley) 15
'Plain-fingered' notes 70, **74,** 76, 77, 82, 89, 90, 99, 109
Plasticine 'wings' **72,** 102, 110
Plastic r's 8, 33, 39, **137,** 139
Playford, Henry 5, 25
Playford, John 26
'Playing in' 36
Plug 30, 35, 40, 105
Portamento **62–3,** 96, 124
Position of hands 31, **42–3,** 46, 47, 51, 119–20
Position of tongue 44, **54,** 59–60
Position of unused fingers 42, 51, 99, **124–5**
Practice 45, 46, 47, 48, 49, 51, 55–6, 57–8, 60, 61–3, 85, 92, 100, 118–19, **122–7,** 133
Praetorius 3, 11, 14, 17, 36, 141
Primitive flutes 1
Principes (Hotteterre) 144
Proceedings of the Royal Musical Association 8
Prophet in the Land, A (Milford) 27
Provençal music 11
Prowo 144
Psyche (Lully) 17
Pulling out **72,** 134
Purcell, Daniel 18, 142
Purcell, Henry 4, 15, 16, **17–18,** 19, 26, 142, 143
Puritans 4

Quantz 21, 25, 120

Rameau 145
Ravenscroft 142
Recorder and Music Magazine, The 142
Recorder—its traditions and its tasks, The (Peter) 61
Recorder News, The 19
Recording machine 45
Reese, Gustave 12, 16
Refingering **70–1,** 100

Registers 31–2, 56, **78,** 110
Rehearsal 128, 130, 132
Reizenstein, Franz 27
Renaissance music (see also Consort Playing) **11–16, 141–2**
Renaissance r. 32, 139
Repeats 113, 133, 134
Repertoire of r. **10–28, 141–7**
Resonance 33
Restoration period 4–6
Revival of r. 8
Rhau 14, 141
Rhythm **61–2,** 64, 101, 127, 135
Ricercare 13, 14
Richardson, Clive 65
Ricordi edition 22, 145
Rinaldo (Handel) 19, 142
Rinforzando 100
Ring, Layton 11
Roman 25
Rondo form 130
Roseberry, Eric 146
Rosenmüller 21
Rosetti r's 138, 139, 140
Rosewood 33, 34, 138, 139, 140
Rosseter 17
Rossi 26
Rossignol en Amour, Le (Couperin) 22, 110
Rothschild, Fritz 130
Rottenburgh 139
Royal wind music 26
Rubber-lined joints 31
Rubbra, Edmund 27, 28, 145
Rudall Carte 138, 140
Runs **76–7,** 86
Rural Music Schools Association 41

Sackbut 16
Sadler 6
Salkeld, Robert 45, 48
Sammartini 18, 143
Saraband 16, 130
Scales 49, 76, 86, 106, 110, 119, 120, **124**
Scarlatti, Alessandro 7, **22–3,** 144
Scheidt 14, 142
Schein 14
Scherer 144

Schickhardt 21, 143, 144
Schmeltzer 21
Schoffer Liederbuch 141
Schott (music and instruments) 2, 10 etc., 41, 42, 45, 48, 63, 64, 65, 90, 96, 113, 136, 137, 138, 139, 141 etc.
Schultz 141–2
Schultze 144
Schumann 124
Schütz 19, 144
Scotland, Music of 141
Scott, Cyril 27
Senfl 141
Shade-fingering **68–9**
Shading **67–9,** 70, 78, 97, 99–100, 103, 110, 123, 125, 133–4
Shadwell 5
Shake 113, **114**
Shakespeare 3, 4
Sharpening—see Intonation
Shaw, G. B. 28
Shaw, Martin 27
Shield 25
Sight-reading 122, **126–7**
Sikorski (publishers) 143, 144
Silberton r. 140
Simpson 142
Simpson, Robert 27
Six Lectures on the R. (Welch) 7–8
Sixth-flute 19, 37, 98, 143
Sizes of r. **36–9**
Slide-fingering **69–70,** 71, 78, 80, 87, 88, 89, 100, 133–4
Slide (ornament) **117–18,** 120
Sling 38
Slurring 45, 47, **51, 56, 62–3,** 64, 74, **76–7,** 78, 80–90 (alternatives), 94–6 (high notes), 115, 122, 124, 125, 131, 134
Sonata form 130
Sophonisba (Marston) 4
Sopranino r. 22, **37,** 54, 57, 72, 98, 110, 137, 139, 143, 144, 146
'Soprano' r. (see Descant r.) 37
Sound production in r. 1, **29–34,** 49, 104, 107
Sound projector 72, **102,** 110
Speaker 1, 30
Speaking, slowness in 39, **61,** 89

Spectator (Addison) 19, 112
Speed of music 102, 116, **130**
Speed of trills 115–16
Society of R. Players 8, 27
Staccato **63,** 109, 131
Staden 141
Staeps, Hans Ulrich 28, 146–7
Stainer and Bell (publishers) 11, 15, 141
Stamitz 24–5, 145
Stance 42, 53, 102, **135**
Stanley 26
Steel, Christopher 146
Stieber r's 38, 139, 140
Still flute 4
Still music 4
St. Matthew Passion (Bach) 20, 123
Stoltzer 13–14
Stopping a note **65**
Strauss, Richard 81
Stress (see also Phrasing) 61–2, 131
Striggio 16
String ensemble with r. 11–14, **16–28,** 37, 38, 98, 102, 132, 135, 143, 144
Style **129–30,** 134
Suddeutscher (publishers) 144
Suo-Gân 45
Supporting finger technique **90–1**
Susato 13
Swainson, Dorothy 121
Sweelinck 12
Systematic Method for Treble R., A (Dinn) 41

Tablature 7, 12
Table of fingerings 141
Tabor-pipe 1, 29
Tafelmusik (Telemann) 20
Taverner 12, 15
Taylor, Stanley 65
Tchaikowsky 26
Teeth, 44, 54, 107
Teeth-ridge 44, 63, 92
Telemann **20,** 25, 64, 96, 98, 113, 127, 144, 145
Tempo 102, 130, 134
Tenor r. 11, 16, 24, 25, 26, **37–8,** 98, 126, 127, 135, 137, 139, 145, 146

Terpsichore (Praetorius) 141
'Terraced' dynamics 101
Tertre, Etienne du 13
Theodosius (Purcell) 18
Thread joints 31, 35
Throat 45, 53, 57, 107, 108
Thumb-book 18
Thumbing 1, 30, 35, **49–50**
    (elementary), 69, **83–4**, 84–90,
    92–3 (high notes), 93–6, 109,
    125–6 (octave jumps)
Thumb-nail 35, 43, 49, 50, 83, 84,
    92, 105, 126
Thumb-pad 43
Thumb-rest **31,** 42, 44, 47, 48, 90,
    125, 137
Thumb trill 119
Tielman Susato 13
Timon of Athens (Purcell) 142
Tin whistle 1
Tippett, Michael 27, 28, 146
Tomkins 15, 142
Tone-quality **4** (associations), **6–7**
    (comparison with flute), 9, 23,
    31–4 (factors affecting), 35, 38,
    39, 40, 44, 47, 48, 50, 54, 55, 59,
    70, 72, **74–90** (alternatives),
    93–6 (high notes), 98, 101, 103,
    104–11, 119, 120, 123, 136–40
Tongue, position of 44, **54,** 59–60
Tonguing 39, 44, 46, 49, 50,
    59–65, 85, 88, 89, **92–6** (high
    notes), 101, 102, 120, 123–4,
    147
Tongue vibrato 60, **64**
Townsend 147
Traversa 6
Trill fingerings (see Alternative
    Fingerings) 75
Trills 41, **75–6,** 79–90, 93, 94, 110,
    112, 113, 114, **115–17, 118–20**
    (execution), 125, 133
Triple tonguing **64**
Triumphs of Oriana, The 2
Trombone 12, 13
True Widow, A (Shadwell) 5
Trumpet 20, 22, 147
Tudor music (see also Elizabethan
    Music) 3
Tuning devices **71**

Tuning holes **72,** 110
Turning over 91, 127, 134
Turns 75, 79, 80, 82, 85, 89, 93,
    113, **116–17,** 119, 120, 125, 133
Twentieth-century music **26–8,**
    108, 117
Two Noble Kinsmen, The 4
Tye 12
Tyther 6

Underblowing 44, **55,** 108
United Music Publishers (Durand)
    145
Universal edition 10 etc., 141 etc.
Unton, Sir Henry 17
Unused fingers, position of 45, 51,
    99, **124–5**

Valentine 18
Vanier, Jeannine 146
Variations 19, 27, 133
Vaughan Williams 27
Vecchi 142
Vellekoop 145
Venus and Adonis (Blow) 4, 18
Veracini 23, 144
Vespers (Monteverdi) 17
Vibraphone 147
Vibrato **56–8** (execution), 60, 64,
    65, 75, 101, **108–9** (application),
    113, 123, 133
Victoria 12
Vigne, de la 22, 144–5
Viol 5, 11, 12, 16, 17, 18, 33
Viola 16, 20, 24, 28, 126, 143, 147
Viola da gamba 19, 144
Violin 5, 7, 8, 9, 15, 20–6, 28, 33,
    122, 144, 145, 146, 147
Virdung 2, 32
Virgin Martyr, The (Massinger) 4
Vivaldi **22–3,** 37, 64, 144, 145
Vocal music 7, 10, 11, 12, 17, 18,
    19, 20, 21, 23, 28, 37, 142, 143–4
Vocal technique 56, 107, 127
Voelckel 13
Voicing **30–2,** 34, 55, 98, 104–5
Volume (Dynamics) 30, 40, **55,**
    60, 61–2, 67, 82, **98–103,** 107,
    132–3, 134
von Heune r's 137, 139, 140

Walsh 5, 18
Walther 12, 14
Ward 16, 141
Warlock, Peter 26
Warming the r. before playing 34, 66, **71,** 93, **105, 134–5**
Water Music (Handel) 19
Wave-length of vibrato **57–8,** 133
Wax 33, 34, 35, 42, 72
Welch, Christopher 7, 8
Wendling 25
'Wheel-barrow' sound projector 72, **102,** 110
Widman 13, 141
Wigmore Hall 27, 145, 146
Wilbye 15
Willaert 13
Williams 143
Williams, Joseph (publishers) 26
'Window' of r. 32, 72, 102

Windway (wind-channel) 29, 30, 32, **36,** 40, 44, 45, 104, 105, 107, 134, 139
'Wings', plasticine **72,** 102, 110
Wischer, Karl-Heinz 28
Woodcock 19, 143
Woods, types of, for r. making **33,** 138, 139
Woodwind Instruments and their History (Baines) 98, 107
Workers' Music Association 15
Wrists **42,** 43, 46–7
Written evidence of existence of r. 2

Xylophone 147

Zeitschrift für Spielmusik series (Moeck) 10 etc., 141 etc.
Zimmerman (publishers) 24

Printed by offset lithography at
Fletcher & Son Ltd
Norwich